✓ 2.95
B & J.

SEMINAR STUDIES IN HISTORY

Editor: Patrick Richardson

NINETEENTH CENTURY EDUCATION

Bell

D1070264

SEMINAR STUDIES IN HISTORY

Editor: Patrick Richardson

A full list of titles in this
series will be found on the
back cover of this book

FEB 29 78

79-493499

SEMINAR STUDIES IN HISTORY

NINETEENTH CENTURY EDUCATION

Eric Midwinter

Project Director,
The Liverpool Educational Priority
Area Project

LONGMAN

WINGATE COLLEGE LIBRARY
WINGATE, N. C.

LONGMAN GROUP LIMITED
London

ASSOCIATED COMPANIES, BRANCHES AND REPRESENTATIVES
THROUGHOUT THE WORLD

© Longman Group Ltd 1970

*All rights reserved. No part of this publication may be reproduced,
stored in a retrieval system, or transmitted in any form or by any means,
electronic, mechanical, photocopying, recording, or otherwise, without
the prior permission of the Copyright owner.*

First published 1970
Second impression 1971

ISBN 0 582 31391 0

PRINTED IN MALTA BY ST PAUL'S PRESS LTD

Contents

53140

Part Three. Perspective

Part Four. Documents

Introduction to the Series

The seminar method of teaching is being used increasingly in VI forms and at universities. It is a way of learning in smaller groups through discussion, designed both to get away from and to supplement the basic lecture techniques. To be successful, the members of a seminar must be informed, or else—in the unkind phrase of a cynic—it can be a 'pooling of ignorance'. The chapter in the textbook of English or European history by its nature cannot provide material in this depth, but at the same time the full academic work may be too long and perhaps too advanced for students at this level.

For this reason we have invited practising teachers in universities, schools and colleges of further education to contribute short studies on specialised aspects of British and European history with these special needs and pupils of this age in mind. For this series the authors have been asked to provide, in addition to their basic analysis, a full selection of documentary material of all kinds and an up-to-date and comprehensive bibliography. Both these sections are referred to in the text, but it is hoped that they will prove to be valuable teaching and learning aids in themselves.

Note on the System of References:

A bold number in round brackets (**5**) in the text refers the reader to the corresponding entry in the Bibliography section at the end of the book.

A bold number in square brackets, preceded by ' doc. ' [**docs, 6, 8**] refers the reader to the corresponding items in the section of Documents, which follows the main text.

PATRICK RICHARDSON
General Editor

Part One

THE
BACKGROUND

1 Education and Society

Educational history is too often studied as a series of legislative enactments, with its students jumping from one Act of Parliament to the next, like mountain goats from peak to peak. This tends to rob it of its rich social and human flavour, for, in many ways, our present educational system is a treasurehouse of our social history (**1, 4**). No logical blue-print produced the schools of today; no tablets were handed down from Mount Sinai in 1944, divinely ordaining an impeccable pattern of education. The system is a mishmash produced by its own history; a welter of years and years of people, laws, ideas, conditions, bricks and mortar, and chance. Of no institution is it truer than of education that to understand its history is to understand its contemporary character (**9, 10, 11**).

Sociologically speaking, education may perhaps be outlined as that which happens between birth and maturity. Nowadays we slip too easily into equating education with schooling, forgetting that, for most of mankind, education has been a question of parental training, tribal instruction and so on. Men, and, for that matter, some other species, have to prepare their young for adult life, and, in many societies this division was clearly marked by initiation ceremonies such as the knight's vow and vigil or the ritual flogging of the Spartan youth. In so far as education is this kind of social exercise, its character is obviously couched in the social terms of the community in which it operates. People, it is said, get the governments they deserve, and, it may be argued, they also get the education systems they deserve. Societies produce, more or less, educational systems in line with their own requirements and mores, and rarely does one find a system for long out of gear with its social background (**2, 5–8, 12, 13**).

This bold statement is possibly only half-true. Society does not baldly produce an educational system, for, as part of society, education contributes to it and interacts with it. Society is a fluid phenomenon, and education is both of and in society.

TUDOR EDUCATION

An interesting example of this is Tudor education. Tudor society, precariously feeling its way out of the confusions of later medieval life, required strong executive government in place of the chaotic conditions of the Wars of the Roses. External stress, in particular exerted by Spain in the latter half of the sixteenth century, accentuated this need. The need was met in part by the dominant human presence of highly effective or authoritative monarchs like Henry VII, Henry VIII or Elizabeth. They were increasingly supported by a vigilant Privy Council. Its membership was normally less than twenty, and the day to day work was often performed by a trio or quartet of Councillors, and this work was as wide ranging as it was important. The Privy Council acted as a 'strict and prying steward' for the monarchy.

In the provinces the Council was in turn backed by a variety of officials, of whom the justices of the peace were the most notable. These rural gentlemen were expected to operate a bewildering nexus of regulations relating to anything from witchcraft and vagabondage to fixing wage levels and repairing roads. A host of courts, the most famous of them being the Star Chamber, assisted in these labours. Parliament, while obviously restricted by this strenuous display of administrative energy, was also of growing importance. Despite the many difficulties of communication and the like, much of this energy had a positive effect, not least because of a small population, mainly concentrated in the south. The so-called 'administrative revolution' associated with the name of Thomas Cromwell and with the fifteen-thirties, is a theory that has its critics, but it seems fair to conclude that, by the end of the sixteenth century, the constitutional structure of a nation-state, complete with a central, omnicompetent government, was fairly well established.

The politics of nation-statehood were paralleled by a tendency towards a national economic pattern. The age of mercantilism was at hand, with the government hoping to deploy economic activity as a projection of warfare and outdo its rivals commercially. This, coupled with anxiety about disturbance internally, motivated Tudor governments to employ harsh powers of interference in the economic and social life of the country. In political as in economic life, many regulations were more honoured in the breach than in the observance. It was difficult to implement such schemes, and the age was a venal and greedy one, little bothered by respect for abstract regulos. Nonetheless, the attempt was made and frequently, if in piecemeal fashion, government intervention was successful.

During the Tudor epoch the economy became more commercialised. Villeinage was slowly passing in favour of a variety of forms of tenantry. Some areas were enclosed, a considerable amount for sheep-farming, and the old-type feudal economy was gradually vanishing, The social structure likewise changed. One school of thought sees in the Elizabethan age the rise of the 'gentry', a class of successful farmers who undermined the power of the aristocracy, but this view has, in recent years, been subject to severe criticism. Certainly the Tudor century was one of social and economic movement. Cloth and woollens contributed over eighty per cent of the export trade, and, during the century, the need for overseas markets grew, especially as the Mediterranean was often at the mercy of Barbary and Spanish pirates and competition on the Baltic littoral was exceedingly brisk, with the Hanseatic League and the North European countries trading hard and charging prohibitive tolls. This encouraged maritime enterprise in more distant spheres, and allied activities, such as shipbuilding and the construction of ports and harbours, received a boost.

Such maritime trades were further encouraged by the needs of national defence. The fishing industry was also encouraged as a means of supporting seafaring, the key to England's defences. Similarly, a host of small trades received encouragement, such as metal-working, sulphur and saltpetre production, and the flax, hemp and canvas trades.

Thus it was that, apart from the prevailing economic belief in mercantilism, mundane reasons motivated state intervention. Social dislocation, such as the vagrancy that accrued from economic changes, was regarded as dangerous and led to the famous Tudor Poor Law enactments. Other state actions were for financial reasons, like Henry VIII's debasement of the coinage or the scores of royal monopolies ranging from ox shinbones to the transportation of calamine stones. Coinage reform, the control of corn exports, market regulations and supervision of interest rates were other examples of state action.

Perhaps the most notable Tudor legislation was the Statute of Artificers of 1563, and it illustrates the wide interests and anxieties

5

of Tudor Government, including their worries about domestic unrest and their feeling that heavy action was the answer. The Statute proposed to negotiate long contracts for apprentices and other craftsmen and it attempted to engineer a graduation system of wage control. Like much sixteenth-century legislation, the aims were too lofty for satisfactory attainment, but the mood of Tudor governments and parliaments led frequently to such efforts at interference.

And this bustling, thriving society naturally produced its characteristic educational forms. One interesting example is Tudor apprenticeship, what G. M. Trevelyan called 'the Englishman's school'. Its object was, according to Trevelyan, 'quite as much social and educational as it was economic'. As the Statute of Artificers argued 'until a man is grown into twenty-three years, he, for the most part but not always, is wild, without judgment and not of sufficient experience to govern himself'. Thus the master-craftsman was enjoined not only to instruct his lads in his calling but in the religious, political and moral tenets of the Elizabethan age.

By Tudor times these callings were most numerous. The Statute of 1563 dealt with upwards of thirty trades, and small undertakings made specialist instruction a necessity at an early age. Apprentice-ship was essential to sustain these dozens of crafts in their localised settings, and it was a forerunner of the massive technical education programmes of today. In its balance of social and economic training, apprenticeship was not unlike many other educational system, and it is a pointed instance of the possibility of educating without schooling (**2, 3, 10, 23**).

The grammar school, that notable English contribution to the Northern Renaissance, is another case in point. In the sixteenth century there was a grammar school to every six thousand of the population (it is one to every fifty thousand today) and no boy lived more than twelve miles from one. They met a secular need, succinctly expressed in Thomas Elyot's *The Governour*, for clerks for the growing commercial and administrative functions of the Tudor state. There was an added vocational demand for agricultural surveyors, architects and builders, accountants and navigators, in the exciting world of sheep enclosures and other agrarian developments, brisk trade and maritime enterprise. Hence mathematics received its initial major boost, for, as John Newton, a Tudor educationist, remarked 'it is the want of mathematical learning in school that makes us weak at sea' (25).

Latin, however, remained the staple diet of the Tudor grammar-schoolboy, and only in a few schools, like Eton and Harrow, was the Latin relieved by a little Greek—Richard Mulcaster, head of the Merchant Taylors' and St Paul's Schools attempted to introduce English into the timetable, but, in the main, modern languages played no part. In many grammar schools the doors were open to boys from differing social grades, and, day by day, they translated Latin pieces and wrote Latin verse or prose. It would be wrong to regard this emphasis on Latin as purely obscurantist. As with much of secondary education today, it was the universities who determined the syllabus, and Oxford and Cambridge demanded this classical grounding. The legal system, with its professional training organised by the Inns of Court, made a similar demand. Latin was still widely used in official and professional circles, and even the local government officers and merchants' accountants in quite small towns would require a grounding in Latin. Nonetheless, one might sympathise with Roger Ascham, most humane and wise of Tudor educationists, in his yearning for an education that furnished boys with 'courtly exercises and gentlemanlike pastimes'. Many grammar-school products were, he claimed, 'great lubbers: always learning and little profiting'.

But there was also an emphasis on conformity, and the grammar schools taught loyalty to monarchy and church, just as the apprentice-masters were expected to watch over the social discipline of their charges. The Schoolmaster's Oath vowed allegiance to the Queen and accepted her supremacy in church matters, and bishops visited schools to seek out 'lewd schoolmasters'. A supposedly compulsory element in every curriculum was a study of Christopher Ocland's *Anglorum Praelia* and *Elizabetha*, two works which, in rhymed hexameters, traced England's recent history to a peaceful and happy consummation in the reign of Queen Elizabeth. Conformity tends, especially in the later years of the Tudor epoch, to be a negative attitude, in that avoidance of unacceptable political and religious poses was often sufficient.

This latitudinarian approach was vital in allowing Puritanism to make its contribution. On the whole, the differences between Puritan and Orthodox Anglican were small compared with the general abhorrence of Catholicism, identified, of course, with Spain, the

7

arch-enemy. The Reformation and the dissolution of the monasteries had obviously ravaged the educational system, and this had provided the incentive for prosperous farmers, merchants and clerics to immortalise themselves in educational foundations. Apart from such personal feelings, the Protestant merchants wanted the products of such schools to maintain the fabric of the community, as clerks, lawyers, government officers and so on. They also wanted to perpetuate their own brands of religion and create the type of society that religion implied. Much of this merchant philanthropy was Puritan in flavour, and, in Elizabeth's reign alone, the predominantly Puritan merchants of London are said to have endowed no less than one hundred and fifty schools.

An early illustration of these various activities was the foundation of Manchester Grammar School in the opening years of the sixteenth century. Twenty-nine pounds were annually bequeathed by Biship Hugh Oldham of Exeter to found the school for 'Lancaster where the children had wits but had been mostly brought up rudely and idly and not in virtue, cunning, education, literature and good manners'. In separate ways, the Renaissance, the Reformation and Puritanism contributed to the grammar-school movement, and, by the closing decades of the sixteenth century, the movement was regarded as one way of 'winning the West for protestantism' (**16, 21, 23**).

This brief résumé of Tudor education illustrates vividly the social determinacy of education. Nor is this confined to the type of education. The agencies of education tend also to be typical of their time. Given the relatively small economic unit of Tudor industry and trade, apprenticeship was ideally fitted to the task of education. By this time trades were as numerous as communications were limited and techniques specialised and restricted. This meant that there was normally a smallish local demand for a variety of skills and these skills were most economically operated on a small scale. A harbour town, for instance, might be serviced by any number of small concerns dealing with shipbuilding, maintenance of port facilities, rope, sail and other sea-faring manufactures, chandlery and other services, and possibly with navigational instruments, metal-working for cannon and chemical products for explosives. The extractive industries, now beginning to grow in importance, were also operated by small groups and, indeed, the concept of mass production or the large-scale enterprise was virtually unheard of for many years. A master-craftsman would frequently practise his calling on such a small-time basis, and it was a logical extension of this that he should take charge of one or two apprentices.

The Tudor system also illustrates the tremendous force of perpetuation in education. For a variety of reasons education is characterised by considerable elements of conservatism, although it is sometimes wishfully described as a forcing-house of change. Rather is it often in the rear of social change, and it is meaningful that the two great Tudor educational agencies, apprenticeship and the grammar school, (to say nothing of that great medieval institution, the university) are still with us today (16, 23).

This is why the choice of Tudor England as an instance of social and educational interaction was not an idle one. As well as exemplifying the general features of education as a primary element in social history, Tudor education holds some of the secrets of the origins of our present system, and, at the same time, it gives perspective. Twentieth-century Britain has grown from the Tudor nation-state, and education has grown with it. As radical changes shook the foundations of English society, the educational system managed to accomplish the massive contradiction of both moving with the times and standing still (25).

THE INDUSTRIAL REVOLUTION

It was before and into the nineteenth century that the most drastic of these social changes was engineered, when the Industrial Revolution transformed the economic and social fabric of yesteryear and ultimately created the heavily urbanised, heavily industrialised nation of this century (19). Similarly education went through the refining fires of a changing society. Vestiges of the old order were snatched from the crumbling ruins: gradually, during the last century, they were refurbished and augmented along characteristically nineteenth-century lines; finally, they were bequeathed, in many ways a readymade system, to the school-children of today.

The nineteenth century, then, was crucial in that it pressed an indelible stamp on the education of the present generations, and the stamp was moulded by industrialism. The term 'Industrial Revolution' implies cataclysm, but the onset of heavy industry was largely a gradual one, growing spontaneously from the hard-earned successes of the world of commerce. By the eighteenth century the solid community of prospering merchants had created an unrivalled trading position, with one of the finest banking systems in the world, deep and sheltered ports, a first-rate mercantile marine, a host of markets and a stable government.

Opinions differ as to the primacy of these factors. Expansion, both in the East and in the West, and the consequent establishment of colonies, provided England with sources both for supplies and for sales. The lucrative, if iniquitous, slave trade, linking West Africa with the West Indies, is an unpleasantly apt instance of this. Foreign trade helped the accumulation of capital which was so important to industrialism, but the domestic, particularly the metropolitan market, was also significant. Tea is a pleasing illustration. The national consumption rose from two million pounds in 1750 to twenty million pounds in 1880. The inventive wit and the traditional craft of the British also played their part, but, in a short outline such as this, probably the major point to make is that of interaction. Each of the elements in industrialism serves as an encouragement to every other element, and the cumulative effect was astounding.

Gradually England was ousting most of its trade rivals, such as Spain, Portugal and Holland. By the late eighteenth century her only possible competitor was France, whose history was politically the converse of our own at this stage, with grave political dislocation at home, culminating in the French Revolution and its aftermath, and crushing defeats abroad, ranging from the War of the Spanish Succession and the Seven Years War to the ultimate catastrophe at Waterloo. This series of wars had a strong colonial flavour, and Britain was making good her markets, while even the loss of the American colonies was not too disruptive commercially. Britain was the workshop of the world, and the Americans continued their trading. As Rome defeated Carthage as a prelude to her great imperial feat, so did England overcome France in creating her industrial empire, after a century in which France had proved a most tenacious and worrying trade rival.

Gradually free trade was adopted in place of the stricter regime of Tudor and Stuart times, for protective tariffs and customs were scarcely needed any more, as industrialism advanced. The world was the oyster of English trade. English merchants and industrialists wanted nothing better than to be free of all kinds of shackles so that they could pursue their profitable enterprises untrammelled. The state adapted itself slowly to this situation, moving away from the paternalistic and often severe governance of the Tudors. The theory of mercantilism was replaced by a theory of state much more individualistic and much less disciplined.

The free trade movement, with Adam Smith as its high priest, moved onward at only a slow pace, for, although many businessmen were attracted to it, there was also bitter opposition. The dramatic tale of the repeal of the Corn Laws in 1847 is an oft-told one, and it is a many-sided tale. Political convulsions, human suffering, clash of personality and of interest, agriculture and industry in conflict— these are a few of its features. It was the last, the most important and the most hard fought of the free trade contests, as the decision was made to allow corn into the country virtually without duty. In effect, the free trade struggle took almost a hundred years to reach this culmination, and it was not long before renewed foreign competition was to call the validity of free trade into question.

The social and economic characteristics of industrialism are still in evidence today. Population more than doubled from the $5\frac{1}{2}$ million of 1700 to the turn of the next century, and continued to spiral until the present day. Town life became the rule rather than the exception. Towns, both old-established and relatively new, mushroomed alarmingly. Each time the United Kingdom doubled its population, there were towns and cities which trebled and quadrupled in size. The industrial slums, with all their attendant evils, drove black scars across the English countryside, and their dreary remains still mar the urban landscapes today. Blackburn jumped from 12,000 in 1801 to 65,000 in 1851, and in the same period Bradford raced from 13,000 to 104,000. By 1850 there were upwards of 200,000 Irish immigrants in Lancashire alone. Along with these conglomerations of people, packed into the dreadful confines of the nineteenth-century town, went a number of critical social ills. Disease was perhaps the most desperate issue in such places, with inadequate water supply and sanitation, and with many forced to crowd into cellars for shelter. The scourge of cholera was to strike and strike again, and cholera was but the worst of the many feared diseases that afflicted the industrial towns. Poverty, crime and ignorance were other social problems associated with town growth, and though none of these difficulties was new, the novel social milieu aggravated the character of each problem and changed it for the worst.

But the key phenomenon of industrialism was the mammoth increase in productivity, associated with the many well-known inventions of the age, the coming of power-driven machinery and the development of the factory system. Coupled with these developments was the construction of more viable communications in the shape of roads and canals, and, later, railways. Coal-mining, the iron and steel trade, textiles and several branches of engineering were the leading industries, and, whether in mine, foundry or mill, the formula of the factory was adopted. The smaller units of a previous age were bypassed. The cottage or domestic system, apprenticeship, the small-scale groups of craftsmen were frequently overwhelmed by the harsh efficiency of the factory. Large-scale agglomerations of power-driven machines, nursed by an army of men, women and children, sprouted in town after town. There is no gainsaying that, whatever the cost in human terms, productivity leapt triumphantly. By 1833 100,000 power-looms whirred in England's cotton mills, and by 1850 Britain was producing half the world's pig-iron. Rationalisation of the economy gradually affected many forms of economic activity. Some progress was made in increasing the productivity of agriculture, while industries like engineering and the manufacture of machine-tools were often revolutionised. Again, the concept of interaction was prominent. For instance, transport needed various engineering trades to improve its potential, whereas engineering required cheap, reliable freight for its products. This spiral of accumulative demands could be duplicated by reference to practically every sphere of the Industrial Revolution.

On the land, in industry, in transport and in trade, capital was poured into an expansionist economy, and towns grew bigger and more concentrated as more and more people crowded therein to snatch a meagre living in the gaunt, humming factories. The frantic competitiveness and pursuit of profit one associates with the cut-throat industrialism of that age was as rampant as the severe social dislocation and distress it caused. Gradually, during the next century and a half, the material benefits of industrialism permeated downwards to secure a physical well-being for the majority of people that would have been unimaginable in 1800. The physical quality of life has undoubtedly improved, but, in many ways, the social context of urban, industrialised society was, by then, written in, and the frame of our present civilisation was structured. It might be argued that, because the political entity—the nation—and the economic motif—a money economy—remained the same, the Industrial Revolution never constituted a basic revolution. In a sense, the most fundamental change was the social one. The fabric of social life underwent a radical change, and the technical and physical traits of the Victorian urban environment were entirely different from those of the seventeenth century rural scene. The very material of life, like clothes, food, work, furniture and housing, were changed, and social horizons were also altered. Some commentators, for instance, have drawn attention to the rhythm and tempo of rural life being grossly disturbed by industrialism and the urban life. There is a tendency to view the preindustrial age as a lost Arcadian pasture, but, of course, it too had its suffering and agony. Child-labour, for example, was no industrial novelty. Much of the pain of industrial life was due to the necessary dislocation of innovation, and it may be argued that industrialism, far from creating a drastic problem, eventually saved Britain from the profound difficulties of a China or an India (24).

Whatever the moral rights and wrongs of industrialism, it certainly altered social relationships as well as social activities. The Industrial Revolution created the wage-earning class, a vast army of workers in the mills, mines and foundries. Again, the wage-earner and the factory were not new, but their large-scale and dominating incidence was. In a phrase, labour was set against capital. Sometimes the change was personified, for Samuel Oldknow was first a merchant, exercising indirect control over the 'putters-out' who fetched and carried muslin to the cottage craftsmen, and then, latterly, he became an industralist, directly in control of a manufacturing concern. The relatively isolated craft-workers became bodies of the wage-earning spinners and weavers. To complete the change, one may see the 'putters-out' replaced by the supervisors in the mills. This very much over-simplified pattern does indicate the trends in social relations. In classical terms, the Industrial Revolution caused the confrontation of the working- and middle-classes, and this major social change helped to produce a crop of effects, such as the rise of trades unionism and the campaigns for all manner of political and social reform (19, 18).

WINGATE COLLEGE LIBRARY
WINGATE, N. C.

INDUSTRIALISM AND PUBLIC EDUCATION

Of all the social modifications consequent on the Industrial Revolution none has proved more comprehensive nor more decisive than the growth of public education for all. Beginning practically from scratch in 1800, the idea and practice of a state education system has developed until today the state annually spends some £1,800 million on educational facilities for its children, apart from other huge sums on items like the universities. Few deny the right of the state to spend some 6 per cent of the gross national product on education or of its rights to enforce school attendance, yet both propositions would have been bitterly contested a century ago. Today there is a constant debate on the quality of education and a constant emphasis on its value to the country for all manner of reasons, ranging from the economic and sociological to the cultural and moral. Education is seen as a plank in the Welfare State, and, in so far as we all must taste its pleasures, it is one of the common denominators of national life. It is regarded by some as a major growth industry and it is, needless to say, a controversial political issue.

Napoleon, it used to be said, was the child of the French Revolution. Public education, it may be argued, was the child of the Industrial Revolution, at least in its social aspects. It was no mere coincidence that, as the industrial society expanded, so did public education expand, in one direction to include more and more children, in another direction to include them for an increasingly longer period and to a higher standard (**30–32**).

In a work of this length it would be impossible to deal even skimpily with the array of possible educational subjects, such as the universities, teacher-training, further education, independent education, technical instruction, adult classes and so on. It has been decided, in the main, to pursue the theme of public education against its social context, concentrating on the development of a state-ordered system of schooling for all children. In 1800 the state had no say in and gave no help to any school. In the nineteen-sixties the state, together with its partners the local education authorities, has administrative and financial authority over primary and secondary schools. In most other social services, central and local government had always had an interest, however slight. One thinks of the poor law or the police forces. It is difficult to offer another example of a major social service with scarcely any pre-cedents before the Industrial Revolution. But the education system sprang, as it were, from feeble roots, and its flowering is, despite the many defects which could be pointed out, one of the inescapable, self-evident facts of modern life.

Stage by stage, the edifice was built. At first the state did little or nothing. Then it encouraged by grants and checked by inspectors. Then it set up *ad hoc* committees to provide for poorly covered areas. Finally, right at the end of the nineteenth century, it adopted the principle of a uniform pattern. That is the substance of the narrative, but, before beginning this account of nineteenth century education, one must examine in more detail the inheritance of the eighteenth century (**26–29**).

2 The Eighteenth Century Heritage

THE DECLINE OF THE OLD

Under the strain of the industrial colossus, the rigid structure of the British state collapsed, and the novel industrial society was to require new responses to meet its challenges and new social services to meet its needs. A strong commercial class began to advance its claims, sometimes at the expense of the squirearchy and the merchant aristocracy. The old administrative format, heavily dependent on the justices of the peace, was outmoded by the onrush of industrialism, and campaigns for parliamentary reform were mounted. The strong state of the Tudors had decayed somewhat, for it was unfitted to an expanding commercial age whose protagonists wished nothing more than liberty to set the trading world by the ears. The state had no technical equipment to regulate these extensive systems of mass productivity; moreover, during the eighteenth century a deep distrust of state action was bred, for the patronage and corruption of Hanoverian government stank in the public's nostrils.

Gradually the state withdrew from most of the purlieus of power, save for obvious exceptions like defence and foreign affairs. From this point of view, the state could neither organise an educational system, through lack of administrative devices; nor could it yet afford one; nor did the state have any desire to organise such a system; nor was there a firm public demand or feeling of need for one.

So one must look outside the state for education around the turn of the nineteenth century. Most education was, such were the premises of society and the economy, non-public. Further, given the disruption, confusion and disunity arising from the Industrial Revolution, it should hardly be surprising to discover a varied array of educational activities being pursued. It must be recalled that as Jane Austen's pointed ironies of upper-class rural life were being played out, the steam hammers and power looms beat out the rhythms of mass production; and Bonny Prince Charlie's vivid and desperate enterprise ended in tragedy on Culloden Moor years after the invention of the spinning jenny (**30**).

This age was one of transition, and transition characterised its educational life. On the one hand, the educational system of the older dispensation was falling into desuetude. This decay was apparent right at the top, for Oxford and Cambridge were educationally impoverished and at the nadir of their influence. The public and grammar schools had degenerated into a dull formalism. The vitality of Renaissance thought and idealism, which had so enthused the sixteenth-century grammar school, had become empty and sterile. The decline had been so stunning that the new literary and mathematical disciplines had by no means dislodged the medieval classical curriculum, and Lily's Latin grammar, published in 1515, was used well into the nineteenth century. Leicester Grammar School, once three hundred strong, had, at the beginning of the nineteenth century, only one boarder and three day-boys. In 1834 there were barely a hundred grammar schools with less than 3,000 pupils in all (**25**).

The public schools fared better, and remained fixed as a symbol of and entrée into the higher echelons of society. In 1835 it was claimed that Eton did not belong to the age—'the system is gone but Eton remains unchanged'—but Eton stood firm. Soon Thomas Arnold of Rugby was to do much to restore and refurbish the image of the public school. The house and prefect system, with their insistence on self-management, and the emphasis on games, to help lads build character, were features to be perpetuated in most later forms of English education (**36**).

Although outside the state system, the public schools exerted an important influence. They educated many of the men who became the politicians and civil servants and inspectors responsible for public education, and much of the thinking and practice of grammar schools was passed on from the public schools. The Clarendon Commission of 1861 was to examine the nine chief public schools (Eton, Harrow, Shrewsbury, St Paul's, Rugby, Charterhouse, Merchant Taylors', Winchester and Westminster) and it found them indispensable for the upkeep and organisation of the nation and the empire, and the army as well as the other professions were well served by them. During the nineteenth century, several public schools were founded, such as Clifton and Malvern, thereby underlining the continuing demand for such an education, a demand by no means satiated today.

Apprenticeship, like the grammar school, had not the public

school's hardiness in face of changed circumstance, and, while it lingered on as a technical and vocational term, its effectiveness as 'the Englishmen's school' vanished with the end of small-scale trading and manufacture. Predictably, it lasted longest where the economy remained unsophisticated, in building, for instance, and in the consumer trades like butchery, baking and cobbling. The concept of apprenticeship was adulterated as it was used as a cover-up for child-labour, especially among paupers, and many will recall that Oliver Twist was apprenticed to Sowerbutts the undertaker. It was also planned on a communal scale with gaunt, lonely 'prentice houses serving various industries (35).

The spectre of child-labour tends to evoke nostalgic backward glances from the grim horror of industrial England in the nineteenth century to the pastoral peace of the eighteenth century. But there had always been child-labour, and there had always been cruelty and overwork in the old cottage system. And, in bald terms, it had a necessitarian side, for contemporaries often argued that the opposite of child-labour was child-starvation. However, with the new-style labour mart, the protecting hand of government, exercised through the agency of the master-craftsman, disappeared, and schooling of any kind was at a discount.

THE RISE OF THE NEW

On the other hand there flooded into the vacuum any number of experimental schools, with their private character a common denominator. Some of these were organised for profit to meet an increasing alienation from 'the monkish system' of the old curricula. Many private schools were excellent, yet, in a period of unrestricted licence, just as men exploited other men in mills, ships and mines, so there were some ready to exploit children. The unscrupulous consequences of this lack of regulation was denounced by Dickens in his description of Squeers and Dotheboys Hall in *Nicholas Nickleby* [doc. 1].

The same was true of dames' schools, of which there were 3,000 in 1818, or one-sixth of the total schools. Some resembled the cosy nook of well-scrubbed infants and comfortable matrons delineated in Charles Kingsley's *Water Babies*. Others existed in the cellars of the large cities, accommodating children whose parents were at work.

Forty or fifty boys and girls were confined in a squalid basement, with, on one or another occasion, the dame dying of cholera or some other disease in a corner.

Another form of private school was the proprietary school, which, like the business enterprises of the era, was founded on the lines of a joint-stock company. In 1825 the Liverpool Institute was so founded, and is still in existence today. There were also some four thousand endowed schools, with 165,000 pupils. These were frequently residential establishments, and they eventually decayed so pitifully that, in 1869, three commissioners were appointed to revise the governing and curricular schemes of dozens of these schools. The commissioners' success was such that some writers have seen in their work the origins of modern secondary schooling (**30, 34**).

The most characteristic and compelling aspect of private elementary schooling was, however, the charity school movement. The well-to-do were anxious to ensure social discipline, particularly when they saw the poor tempted by such rebellious manifestations as the French Revolution. They subscribed their guineas to procure the moral discipline of the poor through religious instruction. They were also anxious to raise bulwarks against popery, as well as to have the poor obey what has been called 'the great law of subordination'. It was a case of 'bless the squire and his relations, and keep us in our proper stations'. The schools were said to benefit agriculture and the guinea subscriptions were deemed a very proper philanthropic offering.

The charity schools sometimes moved from subscriptive to endowed status as gifts and inheritances showered upon them, and they often combined 'working' or vocational with 'catechetical' or religious instruction. Even so they were attacked, principally in Bernard Mandeville's *Fable of the Bees*, for it was argued that knowledge might inhibit farmworkers from labouring with 'cheerfulness and equanimity'. There was always a contest between those who felt that education would encourage and those who felt it would discourage revolution.

It was the S.P.C.K.—the Society for the Promotion of Christian Knowledge—which was the most successful organiser of charity schools. It was started in 1699 and by 1729 they had 1,419 charity schools with 22,303 pupils. The society organised and coordinated; it helped sort out finances; it erected instructional and administrative procedures and even inaugurated some inspection. Attempts

19

were made to move from the normal part-time teaching to full-time staffs, and there was some move to teacher-training. The S.P.C.K. was the first national body to organise elementary education on a national scale for younger children. There were cruelties—the pupils of one London school had to set fire to the building to draw attention to their maltreatment—there was irregular attendance, and many children did no more than a two-year course (**20**).

The cooperation of Anglicans with dissenters collapsed during the eighteenth century, and the nonconformists went their own way. The effect of Methodism on education is a controversial issue. Some see it as 'a reading religion', concerned with education, while others argue that Methodism, by concentrating on the regeneration of the adult, lacked an emphasis on the child. But there was some revival towards the end of the century as Sunday schools were inaugurated. Industrialism left only the Sabbath free for anything, and it was greedily gobbled up by these schools, normally associated with the names of Robert Raikes and Sarah Trimmer. There were over a thousand Sunday schools in 1797, with 69,000 pupils [**doc. 3**].

By the nineteenth century practically the whole of the voluntary elementary school movement was controlled by two major bodies, the nonconformist British and Foreign Bible Society and the Anglican National Society—fostered by the S.P.C.K. In 1818, when the Committee on the Education of the Lower Orders reported, there were over 18,000 day schools with close on half a million on the rolls, and it might be estimated that one of every eleven of the population was having some form of education, either at day or Sunday schools, and the 7 to 13 age group could also be represented in that same ratio of one to eleven. At the same time the difference of educational provision was very great, and one-quarter of the United Kingdom's parishes had no schools. As one moves into the nineteenth century, moreover, three major elements are discernible in terms of important precedents.

Firstly, eighteenth-century education, and in particular the charity school movement, bequeathed a dogmatic style of religious instruction, firmly centred on Bible study. Indeed, the Liverpool Sunday School Union gave prizes to pupils who memorised the most verses of the scriptures, and, in 1818, one scholar broke all records by learning 5,431 verses. This began the long entrenchment of religious instruction in English elementary education. As there was some fear of the poor, when vocationally instructed, competing for clerical and other skilled jobs, there was a tendency to avoid too much vocational training. The syllabus, oddly enough, had a literary slant, but, as with religion, the method of learning was rote-learning. This introduced, alongside religious instruction, the equally long reign of academic as opposed to practical subjects in English elementary education (45).

Secondly, the charity school movement, particularly during the era of S.P.C.K. influence and before that organisation turned to missionary and publishing ventures, was, in a sense, the first national educational agency. It promoted a central body, with overseeing and inspecting devices, overlooking local committees and associations in their management of schools. Here, in embryo, we see the format that English public education was to take. Here is the seed for the bipartite structure English education was to develop over the next century—a central agency in partnership with local agencies. Today the partnership is between the Department of Education and Science and the local education authorities (20).

Thirdly, the early action of the churches in pioneering elementary education gave them a decisive grip which has never been shaken. The inaction of the state left a void into which the voluntary church schools tumbled. It was the all but automatic response of a society which denied itself compulsory schooling, and, after due allowance has been made for their fears and apparent foolishness, one must admire the men who made so sound a start in those unpropitious days. Nonetheless, the alignment of private or voluntary schooling with religion on the grand scale has sometimes proved unfortunate. Other countries—the United States is a prime example—have escaped the disadvantages of an educational system bedevilled by church versus state controversy, but not ourselves. As soon as the state began to develop its interest in education, there was immediate friction with the various churches. This sometimes dispiriting debate has continued into the twentieth century, and, on occasion, it has placed a brake on rapid progress in the educational sphere.

So, with these bequests of its predecessor in mind, to the nineteenth century (26-30), [doc, 3].

Part Two

THE GROWTH OF
PUBLIC
EDUCATION

3 The Voluntary Schools

THE FACTORY FORMULA

By 1830 the Britain of the large town and the busy factory was taking shape. The time was not yet ripe for a public system of education, but the opening decades of the last century were crucial years not so much for the administration of schools as for the format of teaching.

The population explosion, urbanisation and factory development had their impact on the entire social character of the nation. It is helpful to examine education alongside the other great social issues, such as poverty, disease and crime, which man has always to face. Man's response to all these problems, indeed, the manner in which the problems are first defined, is dependent on his basic social condition.

In early modern times poverty was met by the old poor law based on each parish treating its own paupers either in little poor-houses or with doles in money or kind. Disease was met by isolation, quarantine, treatment in the home or occasionally in charitable hospitals with random bunches of the sick housed together. Crime was met by the old watch and ward or 'know everyone' system, whereby the responsibility was shared among the citizenry with some aid from the military. Watchmen and constables served on a localised often temporary and unpaid basis, and criminals, when not transported or hanged, were incarcerated in small lock-ups or bridewells and, occasionally, in county gaols.

Similarly with education, which was, as we have seen, on a small-scale basis with tiny dames' schools, charity schools with an average registration, in 1729, of only fifteen pupils, and so on. For the most part, but not wholly, the teaching was on a tutorial plan; that is, work was prepared for hearing by the teacher either singly or in small groups. This meant that only one or two pupils enjoyed direct teacher contact at a given time, and, of course, the term 'prep' is familiar to most people, if not directly, then through the medium

B

of schoolboy yarns. It is still, basically, the system used at some public schools and universities today, while the group work so popular in primary schools now has some affinities in that there is again differential contact with the teacher.

The move from domestic to factory industry and the compacting together of even larger numbers led to a correspondingly drastic shake-up in the social services, including education. As the middle years of the century were approached, the workhouse, the hospital, the prison and the school were cast or recast in the factory mould. In making such a generalisation there is an obvious danger of over-simplification, and, needless to say, there were many exceptions to a general rule both before and after. Nonetheless, the prevailing views and practices in these various social fields were at their most characteristic with the coming of these institutions. Efficient and economic management became the key, and the division of labour as preached by Adam Smith, that apostle of free trade, was the slogan.

In response to the new look of large-scale poverty there was the amalgamation of parishes into poor law unions, and, slowly, the large union workhouses, operated on severe principles of political economy, were erected. In response to the new look of large-scale disease, with cholera the dreaded scourge of the century, there gradually grew the general hospital on the lines we know today. In response to the new look of large-scale crimes there was estab-lished not only the more rational county and borough police forces but also the national prisons like Dartmoor, originally used for French prisoners of war, and Pentonville (24).

In education the concept of the large school and full classses taught together was likewise broached. In brief, economic and social coordination produced, to some extent, a coordination of social services. People were pressed together in towns and cities and in mills, mines and workshops; almost automatically, they were pressed together for poor relief, health purposes, punishment and education.

Nor do the analogies cease there. The works manager had overall control of the factory; similarly the workhouse master, the hospital matron, the prison governor and the headteacher controlled their respective domains. The factory was in due course divided into workshops supervised by foremen or overlookers; the workhouse into dormitories under overseers, the hospital into wards under sisters, the prison into wings under warders, and the schools into classrooms under teachers. Factory hands were the inmates of the one; paupers, patients, prisoners and pupils the inmates of the others.

One could go on. The workhouses were segregated according to categories of pauperdom, with dormitories for children, old men, lunatics and so forth. The hospitals came to be divided into wards according to age and type of illness. The prison wings were allocated by class of offence. The schools were streamed, more and more completely, according to age and aptitude. And in the factories there was economic 'streaming' or division of labour. The craftsman who could begin and finish a product tended to be replaced by the machine and its operator who could do one part of a job perfectly and thereby contribute efficiently to the whole. There was a sense in which the school followed the factory in architectural detail. The factory had often been a large, barnlike building over which the boss could cast his ubiquitous eye. Gradually, the separate workshops were developed. Many schools, initially, were vast halls with tiered seating and galleries for the different classes. It was much later, in the eighteen-seventies, that the architect E. R. Robson popularised the Germanic pattern of the central hall with classrooms leading off (25), [doc. 3].

The idea that the teaching unit of today is perhaps, at least partially, determined by the factory formula is provocative and somewhat disillusioning, but it is not a fanciful nor an idle speculation. The proponents of these schemes frequently turned to the factory consciously as a mould for social services, just as, in the present, are there are several ready to manage education as a 'industry'. The schools of the period were much commended for their adherence to Adam Smith. Andrew Bell and Joseph Lancaster, the chief progenitors of schools in that period, both maintained that 'the principle in schools and manufactories is the same'. Their earnest admirer and advocate, Sir Thomas Barnard, urged 'their grand principle' as being 'the division of labour applied to intellectual purposes' (33), [doc. 2].

The extreme view on this was taken by some Benthamites or Utilitarians. These followers of Jeremy Bentham applied the yardstick of utility or usefulness to every law and institution. 'What is the use of it?' was the classic Benthamite question, and it led them to an ultrarational, blueprinting, cost-accounting approach in all fields. Their emphasis on thrift and efficiency was welcomed by many a nineteenth-century industrialist, and they enjoyed a fair measure of success in several spheres of social action. The Utilitarians proposed the chrestomathic (literally, 'useful learning') school, with utility as the criterion of its curriculum and business efficiency as the guide to its organisation. It was practised at the famous Hazelwood school at Birmingham. There were forty-three guiding rules, such as the 'comparative proficiency principle' and the 'place-capturing principle'. These helped lead to the prominence given in English education to competitiveness among school-children, even to the physical location of pupils according to ability—hence 'top of the form'. At Hazelwood the bell rang 250 times a week, beginning at 6 a.m. each morning. As the children were routed on this assembly line, marks were awarded or fined for work, with solitary confinement in the dark as a final sanction. A boy banker kept the accounts of these marks, taking a 1 per cent commission. There is a comic element in this, but it is worth recalling the emphasis on marks, house points and silver stars today (**30**).

THE MONITORIAL SYSTEM

If the chrestomathic schools were the extreme in factorylike schools, the more typical and influencial schools were those sponsored by the National and British and Foreign Societies. The National Schools are associated with the name of Andrew Bell (1753–1832) and the British schools with that of Joseph Lancaster (1788–1838) (**44**). These two were largely responsible for the widescale introduction of the monitorial system of teaching, which is regarded by many as a major revolution in that noble art. It was, in fact, a breakthrough from tutorial-cum-preparatory teaching to the class-teaching, which is still, of course, common. Bell hit upon the monitorial scheme in Madras when he inadvertently found himself bereft of teachers, and it is sometimes called the Madras system [**doc. 2**].

Briefly, it was a pyramid system in which teachers taught monitors and monitors taught children, and its protagonists claimed that one teacher could handle a thousand and more children. There was a slight organisational difference between them, in that Lancaster used a monitor straight to twenty children, whereas Bell had a more complicated structure of pairs of bright and dim pupils and a hierarchy of ushers and assistants. The significant point is that every child was under constant teaching supervision.

Both men used sand-writing, and one of Bell's Madras pupils, rejoicing in the name of Johnny Frisker, was the original expert. Dictation and open round-the-class reading were features of both schemes. Lancaster introduced alphabetic writing on the slate, while Bell introduced the syllabic process in writing, with hyphens between syllables, which is still employed today. Rewards and penalties figured largely. Lancaster gave improving pictures for prizes, and, for punishment, he shackled legs, tied hands to a log behind the back, and even put children in a basket on the school roof.

Despite this Houdini-like image, the monitorial schools met the gigantic rise in population full on, with a recipe for dealing with thousands of children, leaving none of them idle. They were, despite their religious origins, industrial in tone. Samuel Taylor Coleridge described them as 'a vast moral steam-engine', and Bell, himself wrote 'like the steam engine or spinning machinery, it diminishes labour and multiplies work', and spoke of 'this intellectual and moral engine' (**33, 50**).

It is significant that Joseph Lancaster started England's first teacher's training college at Borough Road, London, in 1809. This was a logical apex to the monitorial pyramid, for at Borough Road the top echelon in the monitorial hierarchy could be trained. Borough Road fed the British schools, and, soon in 1841, the National Society opened its college in Chelsea. There was a sudden spurt of such activity, and in 1845 there were twenty-two church colleges. The training college was yet another illustration of the move from the apprenticeship concept. Professions and trades, like industry and the social services, were becoming more institutionalised. During the nineteenth century there were several similar developments, with more universities housing a wider range of faculties and more professional institutes such as medical, legal, art and nautical schools (**45**).

What theory of education was behind the teaching of the age? Educational psychology began about a hundred years ago with the investigations of Fechner, but it was not until the turn of the century, with the work of psychologists like Francis Galton in England, Binet in France and various academics in the United States, that such studies were based on sound scholarship.

29

The Growth of Public Education

The nineteenth-century teacher accepted, in the main, the Benthamite view of psychology. This was based on an earlier notion, elaborated in this country by the philosopher John Locke, that the mind was a blank sheet or *tabula rasa* upon which anything could be written. Given the stimuli of pain and pleasure, training or experience could inscribe on the child's mind absolutely any knowledge. The Benthamites applied their normal yardstick of utility in deciding the most useful facts to pour into the child. This is sometimes vulgarly known as 'mug and jug' psychology [**doc. 1**].

The Victorians literally thought the child was father to the man; hence their practice of addressing boys as 'sir' or 'little man' and their tendency to dress children in adult styles. Dickens, for example, often attributes most abstract and sophisticated thoughts to his fictitious children, such as David Copperfield, Little Nell or Oliver Twist. On the other hand, in the opening pages of *Hard Times*, he parodies the age's obsession with 'facts' in the characters of Gradgrind, Bounderby and the teacher Mr M'Choakumchild. The classic example of a man so educated was John Stuart Mill. He records in his *Autobiography* how his father, the dour Scot, James Mill, taught his son while occupying himself with his job and his philosophic writings. He was the Utilitarian expert on education, and wrote the *Encyclopaedia Britannica* article on the subject at that time. It was an incredible *tour de force*. Having mastered English almost before he could walk, Mill moved on to Greek at three, and, having read the standard Greek and English histories by seven, he turned his attention to Latin, algebra, chemistry, philosophy and economics. He later suffered what we would now call a nervous breakdown, but, as Raymond Williams has commented, that form of education did produce one of the most notable of Victorian intellectuals (**49**).

The idea that the child's mind matures and that it can cope only gradually with various levels of knowledge came much later. It was felt that it was neglect of the mind that left it unformed and unfilled. Lewis Carroll's *Alice in Wonderland* was, of course, a mild reminder of the 'childlikeness' of children. The mechanistic view of teaching persisted, and is still strongly entrenched in English, indeed, in European education. The imparting of facts and their memorisation by constant repitition, drilling and testing has a place yet in our schools, and, irrespective of its validity, it is a view of teaching dating from monitorial times (**26–30**), [**docs. 2, 3**].

4 The State Intervenes

THE CHANGING MOOD

For the first thirty years of the century the state remained dormant. Simply, there was no cheap alternative to the voluntary system which could be publicly organised throughout the land. Humanitarians and supporters of laissez-faire could agitate for and against a state system as much as they wished, but the stark lack of an administrative apparatus remained.

It was, in any event, an era of individualism and private enterprise, when many felt that everyone should be wellnigh free to pursue his own self-interest. It was the era of Samuel Smiles and his bestseller, *Self-help*, which heralded the triumph of the self-made man. It was an era when, despite frightening waves of crime, men were worried that to form a police force would inhibit freedom. Attempts to control disease, to coordinate the new types of transport such as canals, railways and macadamised roads, and even to start fire brigades were viewed with suspicion and as anathema. It was hardly surprising that, with the private sector of life so large, education facilities were also privately owned. To have spent public money on education or to have forced children to attend schools would have been regarded as infringements of liberty [**doc. 4**].

It is normally agreed that educational finance often resides in the margin of public finance, and that education suffers as soon as general cuts in expenditure are mooted. The industrial revolution was not sufficiently on its feet to make available resources huge enough to maintain a thorough system. Another point has already been mentioned; namely, the impossibility of keeping the economy going and yet release children for schooling. The Newcastle Commission on Education, speaking in 1858 of 'the perempory demands of the labour market', was convinced that 'if the wages of the child's labour are necessary either to keep the parents from the poor rates or to relieve the pressure of severe and bitter poverty, it is far better that it should go to work' [**doc. 6**].

This short analysis might suggest that certain converse conditions are the prerequisites of growth in the public sector of education. For ease of reference these preconditions may be termed necessity, availability and capability, and over the years it seems, in retrospect, that some compound of these three factors is essential for an advance in state education.

In the first place, advance is difficult until the country needs better-educated citizens to maintain the economy and sustain the social fabric. In other words, as economic functions become more elaborated and as social life becomes more sophisticated, a higher standard of education is required. In the second place, advance is difficult until the country can make available the manpower and money to implement educational schemes. When resources are more forthcoming and when the economy does not need its labour force until they are older, there is a corresponding increase in opportunity for educational growth. In the third place, advance is difficult until the country is capable of managing and administering a system of education. Thus growth in education must often wait on reforms in central and local government.

A negative underlining of these propositions was the long list of vain attempts to involve public authorities and monies before the time was ripe. In 1796, 1797, 1807, 1820 and 1833 there were bills to promote parish schools, but they came to nothing, a failure not unconnected with the unreformed nature of Parliament.

Between 1830 and 1870, however, the mood was changing, as England's political and economic situation crystallised and the bad dream of the French Revolution was forgotten. It was an epoch of transition in the field of social reform. The state became what has been called a tutelary state. The authorities did not interfere with force or positive action; rather did they try to tutor the people into an awareness of their own best interests. In practice this involved the celebrated preventive principle, used most austerely and eagerly by Edwin Chadwick, the famous Benthamite and Victorian bureaucrat. In so far as there was, for instance, too much crime, disease or poverty, people were obstructed from a pursuit of self-help or individualism. They were halted by cholera or theft, or by their substance being wasted away in poor rates.

Chadwick and his acolytes were anxious to keep the ring clear, as he put it, for everyone to enjoy liberty. The state, paradoxically, was to act to reduce interference, just as it might act to reduce tariffs and customs and thereby foster free trade. Hence there were moves to fight poverty, disease and crime by more rational and efficient methods, such as improved drainage and more effectual administration (**24**).

Ignorance was as much a liability as poverty or ill-health, and it was in this atmosphere that the state took its first halting steps. Direct action by the state was as yet unthinkable, but there was every justification for encouraging voluntary bodies who were concerned with the war on ignorance. Other reforms played their part. The reform of the poor law in 1834 caused a rise in pauper schools, and by 1854 34,000 of the 300,000 pauper children were on registers in such schools. Again, the Factory Acts began to have an influence. The first main Factory Act of 1833 required working children between nine and thirteen years of age to have two hours schooling daily, and the 1844 Act increased this to half-a-day. There were, of course, all manner of difficulties with employers and parents, and Leonard Horner, one of the first factory inspectors, found one class operating in a coal cellar (**35**), [**doc. 4**].

Two further advantages accrued from these influences. Firstly, the reforms in public health, police work, prisons, the poor law and factories threw up the idea of the inspector, shifting round on an itinerant basis to investigate the effectiveness of the agency in question. This device was quickly and hungrily seized upon by educational authorities, and Her Majesty's Inspectors are very much part of contemporary educational life. The concept of the inspector is a typically Utilitarian one, with its anxiety to check everything and ensure the tax-payers are getting their money's worth (**43**).

Secondly, and equally characteristic of the Utilitarians' rationalising mind, was the appetite for statistics, a science which grew incredibly over this period. Disraeli is reputed to have quipped that statistics should be used as a drunken man used a lamppost—for support and not for illumination. Nonetheless, vast agglomerations of figures helped the reforms of the age. The registration of births, deaths and marriages, commenced in the reformed Parliament of the eighteen-thirties, is an instance of this. As factory and education statutes increased, it was essential to have some legal check on ages, otherwise there was abuse and negligence (**doc. 4**].

GRANTS AND INSPECTIONS

But more encouragement for education was forthcoming in the radical mood of the eighteen-thirties, with the state anxious to promote local and private initiative for public well-being. In 1833 a Bill, presented by the radical M.P. Roebuck, for local committees to organise schools was rejected, £10,000 each to the National Society and British and Foreign Bible Societies to pay for half the cost of school buildings. The vote in the House of Commons was only fifty to twenty-six in favour, and, by way of contrast, it may be added that, on his marriage to Queen Victoria, Prince Albert received a grant of £80,000.

There was much less parliamentary diffidence in 1839 when a committee of the Privy Council was set up by royal prerogative 'for the consideration of all matters affecting the education of the people' and 'to superintend the application of any sums voted by parliament'. A protest vote was only lost by 275 to 280, and the grant for that year was passed by only two votes. The first secretary of this committee was Dr James Kay-Shuttleworth (1804–77). Significantly, he had been an assistant poor law commissioner and a disciple of Chadwick. He was the author of the *Moral and Physical Condition of the Working Classes in Manchester* and a believer that poverty and social instability could be avoided by education. 'The preservation of internal peace', he said, 'not less than the improvement of our national institutions, depends on the education of the working class' (**39, 44, 50**), [**doc. 5**].

This kind of thinking was very much geared to the mood of the age, and Brian Simon, the noted educational historian, recently described it as 'economic indoctrination' (**30**). There was a strong conviction that education should be used to improve character so that the lower orders would work harder and be less obstreperous. As Lord John Russell, later to become prime minister, wrote in 1839 when the Privy Council committee was established, 'by combining moral teaching with general instruction the young may be saved from the temptations to crime'. It was akin to the philosophy of the charity school, and there is still a similar element in educational thinking.

The committee continued its work, although the vice-president in charge of Her Majesty's Inspectors was also responsible for rinderpest in imported livestock. But it was a start, and, indeed, the forerunner of the Department of Education and Science. From 1856 the Department of Science and Art, supposed to encourage further education, was included in the vice-president's thrall. The grant became an annual one, payable, after 1847, to societies other than the leading two. By 1858 it had risen rapidly to £700,000. To place this in perspective, £24 million were spent on defence that year—a ratio not unlike the nineteen-sixties. As for the H.M.I.s, by far the most influential was Thomas Arnold's son, Matthew, the poet and critic (**37, 38**).

Kay-Shuttleworth was keen to further teaching-training, but his plan for a state college foundered on the sharp rocks of religious controversy. With E. C. Tuffnell, another assistant poor law commissioner, he did, however, establish the Battersea Normal School in 1845, although this was taken over by the National Society and later amalgamated with St Mark's College.

In 1846 Kay-Shuttleworth was instrumental in inaugurating the pupil-teacher system. This was a five year apprenticeship for youths from thirteen to eighteen years of age. Each day the pupil-teacher performed five and a half hours teaching and each week he or she received seven and a half hours instruction. Given the failure of a state college scheme, it fell back on the dying concept of apprenticeship, and, like the church teacher-training colleges, it was a rationalisation of the monitorial idea. It was also, in effect, a form of secondary education for pupils who could manage a higher grade of work but had no schools to attend.

At the end of their apprenticeship, the pupil-teachers could compete for Queen's scholarships which gave entry to a three-year training college course. Unsuccessful candidates were normally found minor posts in the civil service. The scheme began with 200 pupil-teachers, but in 1861 they numbered 14,000. By then there were thirty-five training colleges, seventeen male, fourteen female and, remarkably for the Victorian era, four mixed. Only seven of the thirty-five were not Anglican. Just over two thousand were in attendance at these colleges, an average of sixty in each, which gives an indication of their smallness. They began to receive grants-in-aid from the state, subject, of course, to the usual forms of inspection. In 1861 £50,000 of their total expenditure of £95,000 was state grants. In the same year, 1,676 of the 2,065 on the rolls were Queen's scholars—a tribute to the value of the pupil-teacher scheme. It can be calculated that £50 per head was annually spent on each training college student, which, at a time when the average police-man would count himself lucky to earn so much in a year, was fairly generous. By Stipends during apprenticeship and Queen's scholar-ships, the state thus gave a boost to the teaching profession, and the pupil-teachers, although oft derided, gave enormous solidity and devoted service to English elementary education (27, 29) [doc. 5].

This was, however, as much as the state could handle, given its lack of know-how, its faint interest, and the fiery issues of individu-alism and religion. By 1847 England moved into the political epoch sometimes known as the confusion of the parties. The Conservatives, split asunder by issues like the free trade question, and the Whigs, undergoing a process of realignment, were to emerge as the modern Conservative and Liberal parties led by Disraeli and Gladstone respectively. But, for twenty and more years, there was a seething political disorder which precluded a settled educational policy. Indeed, this political turmoil was one of the reasons for the vastly differing outlooks on education.

Of the main factions there were, firstly, the voluntaryists, based on the Congregational Board of Education, who were eager to keep the state emancipated from education, on the grounds that religion and education are indissoluble, and that state action degrades both. Opposed to them were the secularists, of whom Richard Cobden was perhaps the most notable. They argued that the voluntary system was too fitful, and that a local, not a national, scheme for free education on the rates and without religious ties was feasible. They were encouraged by the success of the similar pioneer Mas-sachusetts system in the United States, and American education continued to develop along secular, state by state lines.

Then there were the denominationalists who liked the idea of using the rates, but felt that only church schools should benefit. Quakers and Roman Catholics were quick to object to this. Lastly, there were the committee of the Privy Council supporters who were pleased with the indirect stimulant to voluntary action already employed by the state (38).

A mixture of the first and last of these groupings held the fort, namely voluntary schools plus state encouragement. There was little local action, for most towns had problems enough at this time without adding education to the agenda. Liverpool was the only town to experiment. In 1827 two interdenominational municipal schools were established, and they were, in fact, England's first local government schools, both of which are still in use. They were rightly regarded as 'a feeler of the national pulse', but the Liberal majority on the council was replaced by a Conservative one in 1841 when fourteen such schools were being planned. The Anglicans led a fierce opposition to these schools, and, in effect, drove out the Roman Catholic pupils. It is arguable that Lord John Russell was deterred from supporting council schools on a national scale by the passion of this opposition, for, as the Bishop of London said, 'the church is the authorised and recognised organ and instrument of national education' (42).

Hereby Liverpool lost its chance to give a national lead to Manchester, which had sprung to prominence at this stage as a thriving cultural, political and economic centre. Asa Briggs succinctly called it 'the shock-city of the eighteen-forties'. With its *Manchester Guardian* and the advanced politico-economic thinkers of the Manchester School, it took a defininite lead in the education movement. The famous Manchester and Salford Education Bill was the test-case for a secular, rate-covered system. Manchester tried out Bills in 1850 and 1853, and, in 1855, three attempts were made.

The situation was one of dilemma. Voluntary schools could no longer support themselves if full results were to be obtained, yet people objected to rates and taxes going to private religious bodies. To resolve the complex problem the Newcastle Commission reported in 1861 on elementary education in England and Wales. This was the first comprehensive review of the nation's educational facilities.

Over $2\frac{1}{2}$ million were on the rolls; over $1\frac{1}{2}$ million in aided and some 860,000 in unaided schools. Between 1839 and 1860 government grants had totalled £$5\frac{1}{2}$ million, only 4 per cent of the poorer classes were obtaining no education, and average schooling was four years. The commission concluded that the grants system was working well enough but that a more efficient organisation was required [doc. 6].

In 1862, therefore, Robert Lowe, the vice-president of the council, introduced the rigorous device of the Revised Code, propounding the notorious principle of payment by results. In order to encourage high and regular attendance and keep a careful fiscal check, he legislated that grants, instead of being of a more general nature, should be based on attendance plus examination by inspectors. It was a characteristically Victorian solution, described by Lowe in typical terms: 'Hitherto we have been living under a system of bounties and protection. Now we propose to have a little free trade.' And again: 'if it is not cheap, it shall be efficient; it if is not efficient, it shall be cheap' (**50**).

It had shortcomings. Teaching became a mechanical and formal concentration on the three 'R's' and it led to that suspicious cold war between teachers and inspectors which is very much part of teaching folklore (**43**). Teacher-training went into stagnation, and the number of pupil-teachers fell [**docs. 7, 9**].

To an extent, nonetheless, it worked, and lasted, albeit in changed forms, until 1897. Average attendance was boosted from 888,000 in 1862 to over a million in 1866, while the grant fell from just over £800,000 to a little over £600,000. Robert Lowe did demonstrate the stark economic facts of educational life, in that he shunned the mealy-mouthed platitudes about schooling and concentrated on its realities. As long as the public acquiesced in child-labour, the three 'R's' were deemed adequate, and few children stayed at school beyond the age of thirteen. Payment by results, obviously enough, was a logical development of the Benthamite idea, and subjected education to the yardstick to which the Victorian expected his business to be subjected.

By the late eighteen-sixties England's unique industrial and trading position was being threatened, and there were political as well as economic rumblings at home. It was with this haphazard collection of voluntary church schools, overlaid by an often soul-destroying state aid, that England prepared to face the challenge of the century's closing decades (**26–29**), [**docs. 4–7, 9**].

5 'Filling the Gaps'

COLLECTIVISM AND EDUCATION

Gradually the state was forced more and more to intervene to redress the ills that beset its citizens. The transitional phase of the state helping individuals and private bodies gave way to a more full-blooded belief in state interference. The state moved from negative protection to positive assistance, and collectivism—the belief that the state is, in some areas, a fitter judge of interests than the individual—became the working creed of English politics. Slowly and imperceptibly the state's power expanded, till in retrospect one may see that by 1900 the balance between individualism and collectivism favoured the latter.

Many factors combined to create the milieu in which collectivism grew. The growth of trade unionism and the extension of the working-class franchise; the social radicalism of some branches of Christianity, notably among nonconformists; the permeation of the material fruits of industrialisation through to the lower levels of society; philosophic attacks from several quarters on the old laissez-faire doctrine—these were but four such factors. Commercial activities became evermore large-scale and involved in high finance. The day of the selfmade man tended to be replaced by the day of the corporation. The government's economic legislation grew in a number of ways, such as railway and company legislation. With industrial competition there was talk of protective tariffs, while, during the scramble for colonies in Africa and Asia, the army and navy played an active and heroic role.

The state's activities in the social field grew tremendously with a rash of Factory Acts, Public Health Acts and the like. Alongside the state, local government began to indulge in a plethora of municipal activities from water and markets to libraries and parks. The Benthamite formulae of utility and of the greatest happiness for the greatest possible number were at hand as useful criteria of collectivist action. Their valuable administrative mechanics, like inspection, the dichotomy of central and local agencies, cost-accounting and the use of expertise, had been forged in the middle years of the century. They were now ready for the intensified tasks of the later years.

Although collectivism has moved forward with inexorable and unresting impetus, three major waves or high water marks may be defined. They are the Gladstonian Liberal legislation and some Conservative legislation in the eighteen-seventies; the Liberal reforms, usually associated with Lloyd George in the years preceding the first world war; and the so-called 'silent revolution' of 1870 to 1950, when the first majority Labour administration established the welfare state. And it is no coincidence that each wave included one of the three seminal Education Acts of 1870, 1902 and 1944. Nowhere is the character of collectivism more patently evident than in public education. The concept that education should be compulsory and gratuitous has the collectivist hallmark, for it begins with the basic presupposition that the state has an obligation to ensure that its citizens are educated. Nowhere is the reversal of views from individualism to collectivism more noticeable than in education. In 1860 many parents would have bitterly resented their children being forced to attend school. In 1960 most parents would passionately denounce any attempt to thwart them.

The story of English education from 1870 onwards is the story of more and more encroachment by the state (**31**). As the state strengthened its hold over the individual, so did it tighten its grip on his education. Not content with supervising the normal years of schooling, it extended its interest gradually to secondary and further education, to university and advanced education of all kinds, and even, at the other extreme, to pre-school nursery education. Now education stands as part of the Welfare State, as part of the grand scheme for providing for everyone from cradle to grave. Education, which in 1830 cost the country nothing, is by now the most expensive social service, and the Education Act of 1870 was the first and, because the first, perhaps the most important step towards a full system of public education (**48, 49**), [**docs. 8, 10**].

The 1870 Act came in an atmosphere of some despair over England's destiny. The 1851 Great Exhibition at the Crystal Palace was intended to parade England's scientific and cultural glories, but it led to misgivings at the onset of foreign competition (**38**).

Richard Cobden warned that 'the very security, trade and the progress of a nation' were heavily reliant on education. By the Paris Exhibition of 1867 the mood was even more desperate, for some British goods looked little less than pathetic beside Belgian, German and American competition. The United States was particularly high-vaunting, outselling Great Britain in many overseas markets and even forcing itself into the home market. A flood of inventions cascaded across the Atlantic, and, with items like Singer's sewing-machines, the technological influence of America on Europe was well under way. A kind of industrial backlash began to operate, as the United States, having struggled from primitive conditions with the aid of European technology, was now repaying the debt boldly and swiftly (25).

Many leaders of trade and industry noticed how, in Germany and France, elementary education provided a pool of labour ready to handle delicate mechanical tasks, assume supervisory roles as foremen and further their technical studies at a higher grade. The increasing sophistication of industry had two relating effects—children were not needed as much and adults who could read and cypher were needed more. Also, the rise in population meant, in some areas, that the ratio of school places to children was worse in 1870 than 1830. In many towns nearly half the children of usual school age were neither at work nor at school. The complexity of industrialism decreased the need for child-labour and, during the eighteen-sixties, a further spate of Factory Acts abolished categories of child-labour. The decade was one of workless, schoolless children. The industrial machines had overtaken their minders, and thousands of children were committed to enforced leisure. And, finally, the 1867 Reform Act enlarged the franchise, notably to include the urban worker. In Robert Lowe's frequently misquoted words, 'it will be absolutely necessary to compel our future masters to learn their letters'.

Birmingham had replaced Manchester in the van of social reform. As cotton had been the basis for the latter's lead in the forties and fifties, so was engineering, concentrated in famous firms like Birmingham Small Arms, to be the basis for the former's vigorous leadership in the next twenty years. Birmingham was to be one of the centres of new-style Liberalism and it is especially remembered in connection with the Chamberlain family. The new image of modern liberalism and the brash political flair of Birmingham helped give Gladstone a majority of a hundred for his first ministry in 1868, and educational reform was a high priority.

It was entrusted to W. E. Forster, a well-respected member of a Bradford wool family, a Quaker, and married to a daughter of Thomas Arnold. He quickly established three charity commissioners in 1869 to examine endowed schools and put them to rights after their years of decay. The following year he presented his Education Bill (50), [docs. 8, 10].

THE SCHOOL BOARDS

The Act has been called a 'hard compromise'. Forster was forced to steer between the National Education League and the National Education Union, both bodies well represented in Parliament and the Liberal Party itself. The League was secularist and wanted popularly elected boards to run education on a nationwide basis. The Union was religious and wished voluntary schools to continue with augmented government aid.

The Act attempted, in Forster's words, 'to fill up the gaps'. Six months grace was given to the church schools to increase their holdings. Nearly 4,000 building applications resulted, whereas the normal annual total was 150, and the churches increased their school properties by a remarkable 30 per cent. After a survey of every area in the country, it would be decided by the Privy Council committee on education whether or not to form a school board to make good deficiencies and ensure some kind of educational opportunity. These would be popularly elected boards and sectarian teaching would be allowed in a school board school. As town and parish councils were not subject to popular election, Forster had to erect *ad hoc* boards, rather than extend the functions of already organised local government bodies. Both church bodies and school boards received public funds. The voluntary schools received treasury grants, and the school boards could also levy a precept on the rate. They could also build schools and, through bye-laws, enforce attendance to thirteen [doc. 11].

The debates were long and bitter, as were the school boards elections that followed the passage of the act. The religious issue was solved by the inclusion of a conscience or withdrawal clause—the famous Cowper-Temple clause—but three nights of acrimonious discussion were necessary. A cumulative voting measure gave some rate-payers fifteen votes, and this produced all manner of clever political manipulations [doc. 12].

Forster himself fell between the sectarians and the non-sectarians. The sectarian supporters thought popularly elected, rate-aided school boards would cause the demise of voluntary schools. Their secularist opponents were inflamed by the six months waiting period, and the fact that boards of poor law guardians were empowered to pay fees for necessitous children in church schools, for they regarded this as an additional course of church income. The ganging up of both sides against Forster possibly cost him his chance of succeeding Gladstone as the Liberal leader.

Nonetheless, by 1874, when the Liberal government fell, 5,000 schools had been added to the existing 8,000. There had been an increase in places of $1\frac{1}{2}$ million, a third of these in board schools. By the end of 1871, as many as 300 school boards were in existence. Unluckily for the future, the Act failed to define 'elementary', assuming it to be read as educational rudiments for 'masons, carpenters, tailors and simple policemen'. It merely asked that schools be 'sufficient, efficient and suitable', and, granting the needs of the situation, probably a vague, wide-ranging brief was the most helpful in the short term (26, 27) [docs. 11, 12].

Progress was sometimes a little slow. There were fears of increased rates, of 'godless' schools and of compulsion. There was the normal dilatoriness of administrative avenues and building programmes. Soon two modifying acts became necessary. Sandon's Act of 1876 established school attendance committees under the jurisdiction of poor law guardians in non-school board areas. No child of under ten was to be employed, and children between ten and fourteen had to have attended school five years or have passed standard IV before he could seek employment. This act was passed by a Conservative minister in strange allegiance with the entire Liberal opposition against Disraeli, the premier, and many of his party. [doc. 11].

Factory Acts continued to pile up, and, by limiting ages and making provision for schooling, each Factory Act was an Education Act and vice versa. But there were anomalies, and, particularly in the countryside, evasions were legion. In 1880, during another Liberal administration, Mundella's Compulsory Attendance Act was passed. This obliged all authorities to submit attendance bye-laws for all children between five and ten. Up to thirteen, exemption from attendance could only be obtained by proficiency —the so-called 'dunces' certificate', based entirely on attendance, being abolished. By January 1881 1,200 sets of bye-laws had been compiled [**doc. 11**].

Such Acts were most necessary, for in 1880 average attendance was 71 per cent in board schools and 62 per cent in voluntary schools. Employers and parents, as well as children, attempted to evade the law. The police often acted as whippers-in, and truancy was frequently a grave problem. School attendance officers were active, and even today their successors are known as 'school boards' in some areas. Teachers were not guiltless, and in 1876 fifty-six teachers had their certificates suspended for falsifying their registers in order to procure better grants.

By the end of the century, however, the elementary education structure had achieved solidity. The Cross Commission of 1888 resulted from church complaints that school boards were overwhelming voluntary schools and that the granting system told against them. This inspired the introduction of a special fee-grant of ten shillings per head in 1891. This 'frankly political move' had the effect of abolishing most fee-paying, for it was the voluntary schools where fees were still paid. Fisher's Act of 1918 formally abolished fees altogether. The eighteen-nineties also saw the school leaving age raised to eleven, the first beginnings of school medicine, with Bradford in the forefront, and the first special schools for the blind, deaf and epileptic. Some steps were taken to pry the curricula free from the icy grip of the three 'R's' and payments by results, while standards for school buildings and 'self-supporting penny dinners' were introduced.

It is possible to consider the thirty years of school board achievement just before their elimination in 1902. In 1899 there were 2,511 boards, under whose auspices twenty million lived. There were also 790 school attendance committees catering for those areas inhabited by the other nine million of the population. There were now five and a half thousand board schools, out of a total of over twenty thousand, and the registered scholars in inspected schools had risen from one million in 1870 to over five million, of whom over half were in voluntary schools. The National Society alone ran more than eleven thousand schools. Between 1870 and 1900 something like £300 had been spent on education. In 1872 the state's contribution had been £1 million, but by 1900 it was £9 million, apart from £5 million on the rates and innumerable voluntary subscriptions. Money costs had risen, and the population had increased, but the statistical evidence was encouraging (47).

Less encouraging was the work done in the schools, for the very onrush of children took the system by storm and clogged it with huge classes that overwhelmed teachers. A school of 120 would have one teacher and two pupil-teachers, perhaps fourteen years old. A typical infant's reading card ran:

'Sit on a sod and nod to me. A cat sits on a sod and nods to a lad. A lad sits on a sod and nods to a cat and to me. It is not a sin to sit on a sod. Am I to sit on a sod and nod? No.'

The mechanical attainments of the three 'R's' were conserved, and the formed pattern of primary education was laid, with the daily dosage of reading, writing and maths, the standards with children arranged by age, the emphasis on the memorisation of information, the periodised timetable, the ritual of registration, the status of subjects in the curriculum and many other characteristics date from this seminal era. The school leaving age, set at eleven and followed by an indefinite period of further teaching, was to establish the contemporary primary and secondary division. One might claim that the historical accident of eleven being the earliest year the child, educated in the eighteen-nineties, could start work was to help determine the seemingly educationally valid age for secondary selection [doc. 11].

Similarly the administrative structure of education was being propounded. The embryonic amateur plan of the S.P.C.K. was copied by the partnership of Education Department at centre and school boards in the locality. This also copied the Victorian feature of combining specially formed central authorities, such as the Poor Law Board, with *ad hoc* local bodies, such as the boards of poor law guardians. This duality was to remain a constant element in educational administration [doc. 11].

The school boards, some set up eagerly, some more grudgingly, enjoyed a fantastic range of governance. Some tiny little rural boards were hard pressed to find five members, and of some it was said that they merely subsidised the local alehouse by holding meetings there [doc. 12]. Conversely the large boards proved most avid school board enthusiasts, with London leading the way and pioneering, for example, the central hall school with classrooms off. The London School board soon controlled 343 schools, and, in

45

fifteen years, Manchester organised fifty schools and 139 'departments' in other buildings, and Leeds forty-three schools.

This polarised nature of the school boards contributed to their downfall. Their opponents were contemptuous of the small fry and terrified of the big fish. It was no coincidence that the enthusiastic cities had Liberal backers, while Conservatives were more influential in the apathetic rural areas. The Conservatives bided their time, and the big fish eventually were tempted, as the next section relates, to snap at tempting bait. However, the precedent of a central body supervising local bodies of all shapes and sizes was created. We take this for granted, but it is not an automatic feature, for the French and German systems are much more heavily centralised and the American system is extremely localised. We have this sometimes uneasy bipartite compromise, and its origins are in the nineteenth century [**doc. 13**].

This administrative dualism was matched by the continuing dualism of state with voluntary church schools, although, again, many countries, as fervently religious as our own, operate a uniform, secular system, without the problem of parents choosing church or state schools. Oddly enough, the church attack on the 'godless' board schools stimulated voluntary subscriptions and helped pass on a dual system to the twentieth century (**41**).

Perhaps most significant of all is the impact of this period on the physical structure of education. Many of our schools still date from this age, while many more have been built in their image since. The architectural format of the school dictates its teaching. The classroom pattern, so familiar to us, means, in practice, that one adult and thirty or forty children form the teaching unit. Should one decide that, for the sake of argument, three teachers and a hundred children were a preferable unit, then it would normally be impossible to house such a relationship fruitfully. An obvious instance of buildings dictating policy has recently been noted in terms of the comprehensive school, where, in order to procure educational change, spatchcock schemes for allying different buildings have been occasionally accepted.

Thus the school boards, despite their defects, programmed the route English public education was destined to follow (**27, 29, 31, 47**), [**docs. 11, 12, 13**].

6 The Local Education Authorities

A UNIFORM PATTERN

Once the 1870 Act was passed, the enlargement of public education advanced inexorably. As the economy expanded and as society became more complicated, so did the need for education receive wider and wider consideration. We are, perhaps, misled into thinking of our national economy but recently coming under siege. Francis Bacon had spoken in Tudor times of 'the state's striving for external power' as the slogan for economic effort, and exhortations to save the country by more vigorous endeavours were as evident in the latter part of the nineteenth century as now. The breakthrough of other nations into the industrial arena challenged Britain to a 'most serious struggle for existence', and education was seen as one of the answers, just as, again today, the cry for augmented technical education is heard. Although collectivism came in two or three major waves, the pressure on the state to act positively was a constant one and the resultant activity was perpetual. The Boer War, for example, was to surprise and alarm people by the illiterate and undernourished nature of its recruits.

This ceaseless kind of pressure built up over the years, and various steps were taken in various directions. It was, nonetheless, the 1902 Education Act which was to codify these piecemeal items into a coordinated pattern, and, by formulating such a pattern, construct the framework of twentieth century education. The 1902 Act attempted two main goals—the establishment of uniform administrative structure and the extension of secondary education (27), [doc. 13].

The possibility of establishing a national system was now a reasonable one, for the necessary administrative format had been erected. There had, of course, been excellent progress in the field of office management and mechanisation. Simple items like typewriters, the telephone, cheaper printing and speedy mails contributed to this, but the chief reform was in local government itself. In 1888 the County Councils Act was passed, setting up sixty-two counties or county areas and almost as many county boroughs, for towns with populations over 50,000. Thus it was feasible to embark on a single coverage of England and Wales for any administrative service. In 1889, in fact, the county councils had been allowed a penny rate for technical education, and some had set up technical instruction committees.

In 1899 the Board of Education replaced the Department of Education. It established a consultative council, not unlike the two advisory councils in existence today, and it followed the example of other professions by inaugurating a register of teachers. Robert Morant became permanent secretary to the Board, and it was he who acted as grey eminence to A. J. Balfour, who, as premier after the 1902 Conservative electoral victory, introduced the 1902 Act (**47**), [**doc. 15**].

This Act reorganised education on a full municipal basis. The 2,500 school boards were swept away, and the 120 county boroughs and counties were substituted. They were to have oversight of all branches of education, elementary, secondary and technical. Each was instructed to appoint an education committee to enact the provisions of the Act, including some non-council members and at least one woman. They had to supply elementary education in the old board schools—now called 'provided' schools. They also had to assume responsibility for the secular instruction in the old voluntary schools—now called 'non-provided' schools. These were made eligible for rate aid for the first time, but building costs had to be met by the religious body concerned. The new local education authorities (L.E.A.s) had to 'take such steps as seem to them desirable . . . to supply or aid the supply of education other than elementary' [**doc. 14**].

A completely coordinated national system was thereby introduced after fifty-nine days of acid parliamentary debate and the application of the closure. There is no gainsaying the administrative uniformity it achieved. Its effect was so shattering that its sponsor, the prime minister, said later rather plaintively: 'I did not realise it would mean more expense and more bureaucracy.'

It is normally agreed that the motives behind the Act were, in part, as emotionally charged as the debates. This was a Conservative

Act, and it was designed as such, and as an affront to the Liberals. The county councils were largely Conservative and they often opposed the Liberal-inspired school boards. The Act was partially dictated by opposition to the vigour and enterprise of some school boards as well as to the sloth and tininess of others. It was because some school boards, especially in Liberal-controlled urban areas, were getting too big for their boots that they were attacked. As Balfour's comment indicates, it was expenditure and officialdom that the Conservatives wished to halt. They wished to give responsibility to their confrères in the rural areas for a policy of retrenchment. That this was not entirely successful, that bureaucracy and expense did increase, is an admirable instance of the almost ineluctable nature of collectivism. Given its impetus in the last quarter of the last century, it forced itself onward in the sometimes unwieldy mould of the 1902 Act.

Some commentators see in the passing of the boards a backward step (**47**). The *ad hoc* nature of the boards gave them a ludicrous range of endeavour and scope from the frighteningly futile to the frighteningly farreaching. Nor were they ubiquitous. On the other hand, they were often suited to local requirements, and their members were single-mindedly committed to education. The school board had education as its sole job, whereas the 1902 Act forced education into the general local governmental maw. Education had to take its place along with the rest of the services [**doc. 14**].

This was excellent from the point of view of meeting the normal financial and other criteria of local government, but education became entangled in the intricate web of municipal life. It is interesting that some educational administrators are presently agitating for single-purpose education authorities not dissimilar to school boards.

Uniformity is a misleading term. The whole country was, indeed, covered, but that could have been accomplished by making school boards obligatory. There was, and is, no equality of authorities, in terms either of population or area. Using today's figures, there is a world of difference between Lancashire's two and a half million people and 400,000 pupils and the Isles of Scilly's 1,800 population and 250 pupils. The county boroughs have a similar inequality. Birmingham has one and a quarter million inhabitants and approximately 200,000 pupils. Canterbury has a population of only

30,000 with 6,000 of them pupils. The counties and county boroughs exist for all kinds of reasons rooted as far back as Anglo-Saxon times and even beyond. English local government has long had a confused appearance, despite efforts at coordination. It seems to find difficulty in equating the strategies of large-scale and efficient organisation with the tactics of political identity and action.

The 1902 Act, then, did not make for a quantitative uniformity. In one way it fed fuel to the flames. Such was the fury of local objections to the L.E.A.s that the government gave way, and arranged that boroughs with populations higher than 10,000 and urban district councils of more than 20,000 should be known as Part III authorities. The county boroughs and counties were entitles Part II authorities and had control of secondary and elementary education, whereas Part III authorities supervised elementary schooling only. Some 200 of these were established, making 328 authorities in all. In brief, many of the old powerful school boards like London or Manchester became Part II and many of the old weak school boards became Part III authorities, frequently with little or no change of personnel or boundaries [**doc. 14**].

The dual system of administration was retained. Now the partnership was between L.E.A. and Board of Education instead of between school board and Department of Education. An alternative might have been to complete the school board pattern and then run it nationally like the General Post Office, but the old duality remained firm [**doc. 15**].

SECONDARY EDUCATION

The educational extension of the system was mainly at the secondary level (**27**). On the whole, the elementary stage, up to eleven, was fairly well settled and was left comparatively untouched. The public school apart, secondary education had becalmed itself in the doldrums during the nineteenth century. The school boards had made some admirable efforts to improve the situation, especially on the technical and scientific side. Payment by results had been much moderated by the end of the century, and the block grant, based on average attendance, was replacing the individual grant, based on each pupil's attendance and ability.

In this less cramped condition, more and more manual and recreative subjects were taught. Standard VII was introduced for bright children who moved through the conventional six standards briskly. Higher grade and higher elementary schools became fashionable, encouraged by the Department of Science and Art, which amalgamated with the Board of Education on the latter's formation. Chemistry, agriculture, cookery, electricity, commercial studies, machine construction, animal physiology and applied mechanics were subjects to be found on the new curricula. In 1900 there were 183 schools of science, under the auspices of the Department of Science and Art, with 25,000 students (**25**).

But there was opposition to the onward march of technical and commercial education, an opposition so successful that the advance of such education in those years has often been forgotten (**31**). It was partly clerical, in that the voluntary schools were endangered by the brash activities of many school boards. It was partly traditionalist, for the 'fizz, fizz, bang, bang' of scientific training seemed to Matthew Arnold's disciples to be opposed to the humane, literary themes of the post-Reformation brand. The Bryce Report on secondary education of 1895 endorsed this view, calling for a balanced general education as the basis for social and political stability. There was also another kind of vocational pull for which a more literary education provided one. The minor executive posts in many commercial firms and the lower professional grades, such as solicitor's clerk and, of course, pupil-teachers, exerted this pull.

Robert Morant was a firm believer in the traditional approach, although unfortunately he erred on the sterile rather on the liberalising side of the humanities (**40**). The London situation offered the ripest ground for action, for a quarrel was ensuing in the eighteen-nineties between the new London County Council's technical instruction committee and the London school board about higher education grants. The London school board had certainly overdone the 1870 Act. They had abolished fees for many adult evening classes and spent money which, under the 1870 Act, was unreasonable. Morant saw his chance. He engineered a situation in which expenses at the Camden School of Art were queried, and T. B. Cockerton, the auditor, surcharged the school board for them. In the high court, Justice Wills ruled against the school board, for, as he pointed out, the 1870 Act implied that rates should only be used for children taking basic subjects (**40**).

This upset the school board's applecart completely. The notorious Cockerton judgment led to severe restrictions on school board spending on prospering technical, evening and adult classes. Apart from this, 150,000 children found their classes in jeopardy. The school boards had overreached themselves, and Morant was not inclined to turn a blind eye to their illegalities (47).

A desire to thwart the school boards and their 'excessive emphasis' on technical education helped to occasion the 1902 Act, and a vacuum was created which Morant was eager to fill with the type of secondary school he wanted. J. W. Headlam, a junior colleague of Morant, prepared a crushing indictment of the school boards' feeble, if brave, efforts at post-elementary tuition, and Morant used this to insist on his 1904 regulations for the new county secondary schools, leaning heavily on the traditional grammar school syllabus. In 1904 there were 491 grammar schools (85,000 pupils); in 1925 there were 1,616 (334,000). Implicit in this action was a mild fear of the National Union of Teachers, founded in 1870 and in 1902 with 22,000 members, for they tended to back the newer theme of vocational education [doc. 15].

There was as yet no chronological distinction between elementary and secondary education, It was a qualitative difference, and now all Part II L.E.A.s had to promote some of this higher level work. Elementary schools ran concurrently with secondary schools, and this made the Part III authorites quite powerful, for they ran elementary schools for children up to the age of sixteen. These schools were normally the so-called all-age schools, and from this elementary stock arose the high elementary, the central and the junior technical schools.

When, in 1944, a formal codification was made of education into primary up to eleven and secondary afterwards, the mechanics of the 1902 Act left England and Wales, in practice, with a two-tier secondary system. Robert Morant re-established the grammar school as a state-run school to set an example of propriety and excellence, and the grammar school, with its basically middle-class evaluation, inherited the typically Victorian acceptance of the examination system. The grammar schools, after 1944, were balanced by the secondary modern schools and a handful of secondary technical schools, in direct descent from the top flight of elementary schooling (50), [docs. 14, 15].

OTHER ISSUES

The 1902 Act built the foundations of English educational administration and secondary education. Nonetheless, at the time the Act
was passed, the spectacular and lively issue was religion. The
success of the school boards and the changes in the granting system
caused consternation in the voluntary school movement (**41**). By
now the voluntary school movement was largely Anglican, for many
nonconformist schools had thrown in their lot with the school boards.
The Conservatives were anxious to lend support to the church
schools, for their links with the Church of England were very strong.
They had tried to relieve the church schools in 1896, but the Bill had
been submerged under 1,238 amendments. In 1902 their chance
came, and, in Morant's words, 'the only way to get up steam . . .
in the face of school board opposition will be to include . . . some
scheme for aiding denominational schools' (**64**).

The Act imposed on L.E.A.s the task of aiding voluntary schools
from the rates. This was the first rate aid the church schools had
received, and the nonconformists, especially in Wales, were furious.
In the next year or so 70,000 people were prosecuted for refusing
to pay their rates. The Liberals fought this part of the Act bitterly,
and on their return to office only the action of the House of Lords
prevented them from abolishing all aid, rates or taxes, to voluntary
schools, which would have placed them on a private footing.
Morant, however, overstepped the mark with his critical views on
L.E.A. inspectors, and 'the assassin of the boards' was transferred by
Lloyd George from education to the new national insurance system
(**40, 50**).

The compromise situation of a compound of municipal and voluntary schools, born of the 1870 Act, was perpetuated by its successor
in 1902. The voluntary schools received a healthy transfusion from
the rates which has helped carry them through into the second half
of the twentieth century.

The onrush of children due to rising population and the reforms
since 1870 threw a heavy burden on the teachers. They, in turn, had
suffered, like all branches of education, from the austerity measures
of 1862, when the revised code and payment by results was introduced. By 1866 the number of pupil-teachers had dropped by a
third and only eight more colleges opened between 1860 and 1890
(**45**).

In 1888 the Cross Commission suggested university day training colleges, which were, in practice, university departments awarding degrees. By 1901 there were seventeen such departments, marking the beginning of the universities' interest in teacher-training. Today all colleges of education are clustered round the adjacent university, whose institute of education acts as a focus for the area training organisation, as each such group is now called.

The 1902 Act permitted the L.E.A.s to form their own teacher-training colleges, and twenty-two were formed by 1914. There are now over one hundred and sixty colleges, many of them municipally controlled, but with a strong minority still in independent, that is, church, hands. The development of secondary education under the 1902 Act killed pupil-teaching stone dead, for pupil-teaching had been, in practice, a substitute secondary education. This very much sharpened the need for teacher-training, both because the pupil-teacher system collapsed and because more teachers were needed for the new secondary schools. These colleges also provided a place for those who could not manage, either for financial or academic reasons, to find a place in a university. This especially applied to girls, for the colleges were to provide thousands of girls with an education and a career. The L.E.A.s were a little dilatory at first in getting colleges started. This was partly due to the exhaustion of resources in the extensive new secondary school programme, and partly to their providing local institutions for a national need. A residential college would draw its students from far and wide, without any guarantee that any would teach locally. Nonetheless, with the aid of increasingly vast exchequer grants, the local authorities were encouraged to establish a network of colleges, and now almost every county and county borough boasts such an institution (26).

One point which needs underlining is the extent to which the schools of those last decades of the nineteenth century determined the present pattern. Many schools erected then are still used, but, just as important, the architectural form has proved most influential. Although admirable improvements have been made in material standards, architects have found it difficult, even when they have tried, to break free of the classroom tradition. However much the method and content of education may be changed, education is remorselessly geared to its physical fabric. Buildings once erected must be used, and, in turn, they dictate the basis of education. We are not only physically but also psychologically adjusted to this, and it is salutary to recall that it has a physical as well as an educational element.

This problem has been writ large by the comprehensive school movement, with its demand for a big campus (**61**). Several authorities are finding it necessary to amalgamate two or more buildings in a spatchcock manner rather than wait until funds are available for custom-built premises. And, whatever the validity of the arguments against schools of high numbers, it is probable that they have an emotional content, in that we are so familiar with the school holding just a few hundreds.

By the first world war, therefore, the English education system was complete, in terms both of administration and organisation. The next fifty years were to build on that foundation rather than destroy it and start afresh. There are several county primary schools today, for instance, that have been in turn British schools, school board schools and provided schools. The theme of continuity is strong indeed in English education (**29, 31, 47**), [**docs. 13, 14, 15**].

Part Three

PERSPECTIVE

c

7 The Effects on Society : 1902-1944

Some commentators have judged the 1902 Act harshly. Although mapping the frame of reference for the twentieth century, some of its features were retrogressive. It destroyed the school boards, many of which were thriving; it lost much of the impetus of technical and scientific education; and it retained the thorny problem of religiously-based schools. It substituted the relatively untested county authorities and placed its faith in a revived grammar school.

This viewpoint, if accepted, may help to explain the comparative lack of progress in English public education in the first half of the century. More obviously thwarting such progress were two world wars and the intervening depression. The epoch before 1944 positively bloomed with reports on aspects of education, but more typical of the age was the so-called 'Geddes axe' of 1931 which cut back severely on educational finance.

Despite the international setbacks, both economic and political, collectivism moved onwards, and, as children were an obvious choice for the state's protection, many more facilities were established to succour them. The school medical services, special schools for children variously handicapped, employment advice and improved school meals and milk services were examples of this trend. In 1912 there were one hundred and in 1937 there were two thousand children's clinics. Building standards were raised considerably, and a blacklist was drawn up of below-standard schools. The 1918 Education Act was prominent in encouraging work in some of these areas, and, although never effectively implemented before the last war, this act lifted the school leaving age to fifteen.

In a sense these reforms were social rather than educational, although it is difficult and dangerous to distinguish between these two aspects. Such reforms were part and parcel of the improving standards of life which grew during these years, but they have little purely educational significance, and changes in school organisation were not nearly so significant (**26, 29**).

The grammar schools were naturally expanding. In 1910 only 4 per cent of children attended a grammar school, whereas in 1937 the figure was 11 per cent. And yet, just prior to World War II, only 70 per cent of eligible state school pupils and 32 per cent of church school pupils were receiving secondary education as defined. The rest were still managing in all-age elementary schools and similar institutions. The overall totals of expenditure—roughly £30 million before the 1914–18 war and £90 million before the 1939–45 war—look encouraging, but the population had risen, the purchasing value of the pound had approximately halved, and one must take account of expenditure on directly social facilities.

Oddly enough, despite a rise in population, there was a fall from six to five and a half million in the number of pupils over the same period. This was partially a consequence of the dreadful losses of young men in the Great War. Their slaughter had another educational result. Thousands of women were left as widows or without the chance of marriage, especially those of a social gentility likely to have made them brides for the badly-hit officer class. Many of these ladies moved into the growing teacher-training colleges, and a gigantic army of spinsters maintained the teaching service in the United Kingdom for the next generation. Teacher supply enjoyed a partly false sense of security until the gradual retirement of these admirable ladies occurred as the postwar bulge in the birthrate hit the schools and the wastage of women teachers leapt. That, in outline, explains the shortage of teachers today.

The effects of a full-scale scheme of public education were, nonetheless, manifold. Amidst the complexities of modern society the illiterate was as surely maimed as if he had lost an arm or leg. Controversy rages as to the degree of benefit. A popular item of discussion revolves round reading matter. It can be put as a query about the link between the growth of literacy and the growth of the popular or sensational press (**48, 49**). On the other hand, the sophisticated and elaborate mechanisms operated by workers in the twentieth century and the myriad complicated bureaucratic devices to which the citizen is subjected would be futile and useless without a state education system (**51–54**).

One of the factors which became increasingly apparent as the years passed was the slowness with which educational change occurs.

Once a reform has been decided on, months and even years of administrative haggling and then building programmes are frequently necessary. Sometimes the need for reform has been bypassed before the reform has been implemented. It could, for example, be argued that, by the time Morant's type of education, providing generally well-cultivated young men for Edwardian merchant houses, had been accomplished, the need was for technologists and engineers for the jet age.

Even if this is a slightly exaggerated opinion, there is no doubting the public clamour for improved education by 1944. There was a sincere feeling that children should have the most excellent of educations. People were appalled by the consequences of education in fascist hands as in Germany and Italy, and they were so aghast at the horror and folly of war that they were determined to refurbish education completely. Total war had brought demolished schools and a major hold-up in reconstruction programmes. It had also brought evacuation, and some of the agitation for an Education Act was born of the disturbing effect slum children had on the rural environs.

Again, the nation had become adjusted to the extensive governance and controls of wartime, for the United Kingdom was subjected to a most intricate and demanding pattern of supervision. The mood was for change, and the immediate postwar era was one of continued collectivism, and the erection of the welfare state. It was hardly surprising that education was one of the priorities, and the 1944 Act was passed in an atmosphere of tranquillity unique in educational legislation.

One reason for the lack of controversy was its passage by the National Coalition Government under Winston Churchill's premiership. Its sponsors were R. A. Butler, a moderate conservative, and Chuter Ede, a moderate socialist. The camaraderie bred of a successful war effort was evident, and there was goodwill in abundance. Everyone was eager to build a better world (**26, 55**).

Another more humdrum reason for its mild reception was its non-controversial nature. It was hardly a revolutionary measure; rather did it consolidate and beatify the *status quo*, thereby offering little scope for political argument.

Administratively, the Board of Education was replaced by the Ministry of Education and latterly this has become the Department of Education and Science. The status of the minister in charge of education has improved slightly over the last hundred years, but it is still not regarded as a top-ranking post. Two Advisory Councils for England and Wales replaced the old Consultative Committee which had replaced the older Coding Committee of the nineteenth century.

The bipartite administrative structure begun by the school boards and the privy council and continued by the local education authorities and the Board of Education was maintained. The Part III authorities were abolished, reducing the number of L.E.A.s from 315 to 146. A major outcry in the debates came from the aggrieved Part III authorities, and, such was the good-humoured tenor of the debates, it was decided to have divisional executives and excepted districts within L.E.A.s to whom responsibility, albeit without the power of financial levying, could be delegated. Many a divisional executive has negotiated itself to its present position from being not only a Part III authority, but, before that, a school board.

The alliance of a central and a local agency thus remained, and, although control of education, the dual administrative system is well entrenched. If there has been a change in this balance, it has been, as with all collectivist trends, in favour of the centre. Finance is the key to administration, and the state now provides three-quarters of the expenditure as opposed to a half at the turn of the century. There is little doubt that the chief element in the extension of public education has been financial. Allowing even for changing values, a rising population and material benefits like school medicine and milk, the increase from £16 per pupil in 1900 to nearly £1,800 in 1966 is massive. It represents $5\frac{1}{2}$ per cent of the gross national product, as compared to 1 per cent in 1900. Alternatively, the percentage of central revenue—6 to 7 per cent—is less than the 10 per cent of 1910. Certainly there has been little fundamental increase since the war, and the Crowther report argued that, for twenty years, the money spent on 'the central purposes of education' had only kept up with 'the general expansion of national income' (**64**).

The attempt at a unitary administrative system arose from the sensible decision to abolish the elementary category, and to have progressive stages of primary, secondary and further education. Contrary to popular fallacy, the Act did not advise on the tripartite division of secondary education into grammar, modern and technical. This was suggested in the 1943 White Paper on Educational Reconstruction, and had been foreshadowed by earlier reports. All fee-paying was abolished in state schools, and education was now, in the words of the old Victorian slogan, 'universal, compulsory and gratuitous'.

In reality, the 1944 Act merely revitalised the already existing post-primary scheme. In 1963 there were 1,300 grammar schools (700,000 pupils), 4,000 modern schools ($1\frac{1}{2}$ million pupils) and only 204 technical schools, and even this number is dwindling. The modern schools were substituted for the old pedigree of higher elementary, senior and central schools. Indeed, in 1963, twenty years after the Act, 130,000 pupils were still in the 600 all-age schools. The 1944 provision on a school leaving age of sixteen is just about to be implemented, and the idea of county colleges has remained dormant (55, 56).

The dual system of schools remained. The council or 'provided' schools were renamed county schools, and the voluntary or 'non-provided' schools were divided into three classes. These were 'aided' schools, 'special-agreement schools' and 'controlled' schools. They vary according to the amount of authority and financial obligation left to the voluntary body. In 'aided' schools it is high, in 'special-agreement' schools it is middling, and in 'controlled' schools it is fairly low. In 1963 there were 5,300 'aided' (3,000 C of E; 2,000 Roman Catholic) 150 'special agreement' (117 Roman Catholic) and 4,500 'controlled' (4,000 C of E; 2 Roman Catholic).

The religious issue has remained another constant in English education, and, with these adjustments, the compromise system was sustained. The 1944 Act also gave a fillip to voluntary secondary education, which had not been a sturdy plant—now one-sixth of our secondary schools are church based. All in all, there are now close on 40,000 maintained schools. Remembering that there was, in practice, no state school before 1870, this represents a remarkable overhaul by the state.

The churches have lost some, but by no means all, ground because of the difficulty of maintaining standards. The 1944 Act, in effect, forced increased standards on them by exerting more control and contributing more money. The elaborate bargaining surrounding the Act meant some compensation had to be found for this loss of influence. This was met by the decision to make a daily act of communal worship and a weekly period of religious education obligatory in state schools. This, at least, is one explanation of the decision, for the first and so far only time, to make a particular subject compulsory (**26, 29, 55, 56**).

An analysis of the 1944 Act underlines the seminal nature of nineteenth-century education. Important as the Act was, it is possible to see it as adapting the existing precedents at all stages and creating few original themes. A two-tier system of administration, a two-tier system of secondary school organisation and a two-tier system of state and non-state schools had been evolved by 1902, and the twentieth century perpetuated this. It is also possible, on closer analysis, to apply such an interpretation to other educational features such as school curricula, teaching methodology, teacher-training and university studies (**25, 26, 29, 55, 56, 64**).

8 Education Today

In many ways, therefore, the nineteenth century decided what education system the twentieth century should have. As with any other social service or social condition, it is difficult to break out of the bonds of circumstance and, even if we so wished, make wholesale changes. Progress has, of course, been made in all kinds of material ways, such as improved conditions, increased technical facilities, much improved buildings and so on. The whole atmosphere of schooling is probably brighter and healthier and happier than in years gone by. Here again, however, the standards and the mood reflect the relative prosperity and affluence of the age.

The most interesting modification in school organisation since 1944 has been the comprehensive movement in secondary education (**61, 62, 63**). Although comprehension has a variety of interpretations, the major principle is that, as with primary schools, there should be no differentiation of schools according to aptitude, and that all children in a given area should attend the same secondary school. The differentiation was objected to both on social and on educational grounds, and the Labour Party became the chief proponents of a scheme in which all children were to be treated equally and no once-for-all decision about their futures was to be made at the eleven-plus selection stage. Opponents of comprehension upheld the traditional value of the grammar school and the effectiveness of differential education. It was also suggested that the large units necessary for comprehension schools could be soulless and impersonal.

The comprehensive movement has made considerable headway. The Labour administration, which took office in 1964, requested all L.E.A.s to produce plans for comprehension, and some areas have already implemented schemes. It is interesting to speculate that we may be living in a fourth wave of collectivism, and that, as usual, a major educational change is implicit in it. Such agencies as the Prices and Incomes Board and the Land Commission might testify to this. On the other hand, collectivism at the moment does not seem to have the impetus of the eighteen-seventies, the nineteen-hundreds or the nineteen-forties, and at present the Conservatives, who are much more chary and less doctrinaire than their Labour rivals about comprehension, hold control of a great majority of the L.E.A.s (58–60).

Another fascinating speculation is that the comprehensive school, in its size and scope, is in line with the enlarged social and economic institutions of the era. The proclivity appears to be towards hugeness and even monopoly, be it state or private. Ours is a world of the I.C.I., the National Coal Board, the Thompson press, Granada, the Prudential and the supermarket. It is a world of vast commercial corporations, nationalised industries, huge general hospitals and complex trading emporia. Just as apprenticeship was geared to the Tudor craft unit and the old-type school to the factory system, so there is perhaps a similar link between the erection of the large comprehensive school or the wide-ranging university campus and the mammoth scale of our social and economic background.

In one sense, however, the comprehensive school may only nibble at the problem of secondary education. It has been increasingly recognised that the grand slogans of 1944, equality of opportunity for children and parity of esteem for schools, can prove empty without answering equality and parity in society at large. The Robbins Report, for instance, recorded that, of children born in 1940/41, as many as 45 per cent of those of upper middle-class parentage and as few as 2 per cent of those with semiskilled and unskilled fathers stayed on for higher education. It is remarkable that, despite the admirable opening of channels, with eleven-plus selection, all kinds of educational encouragement and reasonably fair grants, the proportion of children of manual workers at universities is now only marginally higher than in 1939, when few openings existed. Opponents of the comprehensive school feel that, by operating neighbourhood unit schools, some children will be even less likely to make the higher grade than when the grammar school gave them an opportunity to mix with a wide social gamut (51–54).

Looking a little into the future, one might hazard the generalised guess that secondary education might remain two-tier in practice even where comprehension takes roots. In brief, one might have a somewhat Orwellian situation in which the children in middle-class suburbs follow professional and academic bents, and the children in working-class council house estates do not (**58,–60**).

This may well be a gloomy exaggeration, but it serves to underline the possibility of the nineteenth century retaining its not altogether pleasant grip. It also brings us full circle by reminding us of the importance of the social factor in education. Europe in the Middle Ages had an educational system suited to its social needs; equally, modern Britain automatically creates the system of schools it requires. A moment's thought of the comedy of transforming one to the other (the novice knight doing 'O level' jousting?) points the truth of this. This is by no means to denigrate the vital role of other factors such as influential individuals, inspirational creeds, inspiriting ideals, valuable theses and research and a dozen other items. Nonetheless, the economic and social elements are very important indeed.

Their importance helps to explain the mishmash, the random patchwork quilt of English education. It is a lively, organic, fluid organism, and the bewildering mosaic of its characteristics are explicable in terms of history, and it is history which helps one to understand it and thus use it the more fruitfully. The authorities are of all shapes and sizes; there is a delicate set of balances between them and the central department, and between both and the schools; there is a most complicated fiscal control; teacher supply is provided for in two or three different forms and there are four major teachers' associations; there exists a colourful proliferation of types of secondary schools, to say nothing of the new 'middle' (usually eight to twelve or thirteen) schools; as well as state schools, ranging from one-teacher village schools to comprehensives of over two thousand pupils, there are three types of church school, as well as a wide selection of direct grant and independent schools; there is no national yardstick of selection or otherwise for secondary education and several different bodies supervise the General Certificate of Education; and, needless to say, curricula and methodology vary enormously (**57, 60**).

For better or for worse, the system is a non-standardised one. It is, with all the inherent disadvantages and advantages, not a uniform structure. Perpetuation is frequently the key to this situation. At the beginning of the nineteenth century there was scarcely a ubiquitous and thorough system; by the end of the century there was free education for all to a teenage level. The Victorian epoch was one of trial and error in education; it was a swirling laboratory of experiments with schools. But these were human experiments, and, it seems, almost regardless of the success or otherwise of these experiments, practically everything that was tried with any soundness remained. Because of the essentially human character of education and educational administration, it was never possible, once started, to retrace steps or start again. All reform was perforce piecemeal, and its consequences invariably halting and indeterminate.

This overriding quality of English education is both its frailty and its glory. It is irritating, even maddening, in its all but whimsical inconsistency, and yet its very freedom from rigidity gives it the flexibility to flourish cheerfully and healthily and never stagnate.

Part Four

DOCUMENTS

The Documents

An attempt has been made to illustrate the role of the state at each stage in the story of its increasing control. This has been balanced with examples of local supervision, in order to pinpoint the dual nature of educational administration. Most of the correspondence and miscellaneous papers on educational matters are to be found in the Public Record Office, but so much has been published in Blue Books and White Papers that most major libraries have extensive coverage of education in parliamentary papers and H.M.S.O. material.

School board records have normally wound their way to the archives of the relevant county or county borough. Some county record offices have fairly full collections of school board minute books. It is interesting to compare these, often recording the activities of a small board, with the board minutes of a larger town or city. The opening months of the new education committees are of interest, as the changeover from school boards occurred. These minutes were usually printed, and local education offices and local libraries normally keep them.

The schools themselves maintained logbooks from the early years of the century, and it is often possible to obtain permission to view these in the schools. On closure and, in some areas, after a period of years, these logbooks are collated in education offices and county or county borough record offices.

Education is a fruitful research topic for local history students, especially those in schools. The building itself is often a splendid starting point, and its architectural layout is a valid guide to the thinking behind it. In some cases the schools may themselves have valuable records, and many schools maintain a private collection of, for instance, photographs of classes, speech day programmes, newspaper cuttings and school magazines. Some schools have official histories, while several school boards have had books written about them. Others have been the subject of university research, and, occasionally, such theses have been duplicated or mimeographed for local libraries.

the documents

It is worth remembering the obvious fact that education is about children, which means that people in their seventies and eighties are able and often loquaciously willing to offer firsthand testimony about nineteenth-century schools. Luckily for the would-be researcher, childhood is a fruitful time for reminiscence and also for souvenirs, and many homes contain a store of photographs, accounts of opening ceremonies, old reports and the like. It should be emphasised that, significant as administration and organisation are, the real meat of education is what happened in the classroom. Dim memories of long ago lessons, eked out with old textbooks, old reports and old exercise books, can provide a satisfactory picture of the curriculum and teaching method of late Victorian education.

Novels, newspapers and autobiographies are other possible sources. The politics of education, especially in terms of the religious issue, were lovingly reported by the national and local press. School board elections, for example, had full press coverage. Many autobiographers and biographers devote considerable space to schooldays, while the Victorian novelist was much more obsessed with childhood than his modern counterpart. The majority of Dickens's novels offer some insight into the life of the Victorian child—David Copperfield, Oliver Twist, Little Nell, Pip, Little Dorrit, Paul Dombey and Tiny Tim are just a few, and there are as many schoolmasters, such as M'Choakumchild, Dr Creedle and Squeers. Tom Brown, Jane Eyre, Kipling's Stalky, Alice, and Kingsley's sweeping boy, Tom, are other members of this vast gallery of Victorian children. Indeed, the fascination of English schoolboys to this day with the residential school is a research topic in itself. Tom Brown and Stalky were to be followed by Talbot Baines Reed's *Fourth Form at St Dominic's* and Frank Richards' Billy Bunter, and, apart from the scores of such yarns, comics like the *Wizard* and *Rover* always supported their own minor public school, of which perhaps *Hotspur's* Red Circle was the most famous.

Needless to say, the following collection dips only slightly into a bottomless pool of research material.

THE VICTORIAN NOVEL

MR SQUEERS AND DOTHEBOYS HALL

*The Victorian novel provides a constant source of pictures of the eighteenth-
and nineteenth-century schoolrooms, and Dickens's Nicholas Nickleby,
published in 1838, includes possibly the most infamous fictitious school of all
time. Dickens attacked the unlicensed and dreadful state of some of the private
schools which existed in that era of social dislocation. Of incidental interest
is the manner in which, in those pre-monitorial days, Squeers draws groups of
children from the whole class in order, in his own inimitable way, to teach them.*

After some half-hour's delay Mr Squeers reappeared, and the
boys took their places and their books, of which latter commodity
the average might be about one to eight learners. A few minutes
having elapsed, during which Mr Squeers looked very profound, as
if he had a perfect apprehension of what was inside all the books,
and could say every word of their contents by heart if he only chose
to take the trouble, that gentleman called up the first class.

Obedient to this summons there ranged themselves in front of the
schoolmaster's desk, half a dozen scarecrows, out at knees and
elbows, one of whom placed a torn and filthy book beneath his
learned eye.

"This is the first class in English spelling and philosophy,
Nickleby," said Squeers, beckoning Nicholas to stand beside him.
"We'll get up a Latin one, and hand that over to you. Now then,
where's the first boy?"

"Please, Sir, he's cleaning the back parlour window," said the
temporary head of the philosophical class.

"So he is, to be sure," rejoined Squeers. "We go upon the practical
mode of teaching, Nickleby; the regular education system. C-l-e-a-n,
clean, verb active, to make bright, to scour. W-i-n-, win, d-e-r, der,
winder, a casement. When the boy knows this out of book, he goes
and does it. It's just the same principle as the use of the globes.
Where's the second boy?"

"Please, Sir, he's weeding the garden," replied a small voice.
"To be sure," said Squeers, by no means disconcerted. "So he is.

73

B-o-t, bot, t-i-n, bottin, n-e-y, bottinney, noun substantive, a knowledge of plants. When he has learned that bottinney means a knowledge of plants, he goes and knows 'em. That's our system, Nickleby; what do you think of it?"

"It's a very useful one, at any rate," answered Nicholas significantly.

"I believe you," rejoined Squeers, not remarking the emphasis of his usher. "Third boy, what's a horse?"

"A beast, Sir," replied the boy.

"So it is," said Squeers. "Ain't it, Nickleby?"

"I believe there is no doubt of that, Sir," answered Nicholas.

"Of course there isn't," said Squeers. "A horse is a quadruped, and quadruped's Latin for beast, as everybody that's gone through the grammar knows, or else where's the use of having grammars at all?"

"Where, indeed!" said Nicholas abstractedly.

"As you're perfect in that," resumed Squeers, turning to the boy, "go and look after MY horse, and rub him down well, or I'll rub you down. The rest of the class go and draw water up till somebody tells you to leave off, for it's washing-day to-morrow, and they want the coppers filled."

THE MONITORIAL SYSTEM

JOSEPH LANCASTER AND ANDREW BELL, *c.* 1805

This section consists of several examples drawn from various sources of the writings of and about these two most notable proponents of the monitorial system. It makes no attempt to describe the system of their work fully, but the examples catch the flavour of the two men and the spirit in which they approached their work. The Welsh School was a charity school for Welsh children in Liverpool, taken over by the British Society. The Barrington school was in Bishop Auckland.

JOSEPH LANCASTER
(Letter to his daughter)   Liverpool 26th of 2nd. Mo. 1809.

I lecture this evening at the Welch school . . . I have come here just in time to save a noble institution from ruin. There is more danger to the plan from misguided committees and weak school-masters . . . than there is, or ever was, from pecuniary circumstances; and I am convinced that if I had not travelled into these parts the plan would have had a death-blow here. Here is a noble school-room, which cost £1,700 building, capable of holding 600 to 700 boys; a liberal-minded set of men are the committee but all Taffys or Welchmen. . . . The school was three days ago a scene of disorder and riot, now a pin may be heard to drop, and order is the order of the day.

From W. Corston's *A Brief Sketch of the Life of Joseph Lancaster*, 1840.

Any boy of eight years old, who can barely read writing, and numerate well, is, by means of the guide containing the sums, and the key thereto, qualified to teach the first four rules of arithmetic, simple and compound, if the key is correct, with as much accuracy as mathematicians who may have kept school for twenty years . . . . Every boy in each class is told by the teacher all he is to do; and his sole business is to do it so often as to become quite familiar with it.

The more pliable the tree, the easier it will bend; and children cannot be too soon trained in the way they should go. This might be done with double effect in workhouses, as in them the children are entirely at the disposal of their superiors; and there is not much

75

danger of their showing refractory dispositions, as in the case of children who are spoiled by too much indulgence. . . . The mental powers of boys are similar to those of men, but in embryo.—The same stimulus that animates men to action will have a proportionate effect on juvenile minds.

ANDREW BELL

It is not proposed that the children of the poor be educated in an expensive manner, or even taught to write and cypher. . . . There is a risk of elevating them from the drudgery of daily labour above their condition, and thereby render them discontented and unhappy in their lot. It may suffice to teach the generality, on an economical plan, to read their Bible, and understand the doctrines of our Holy Religion.

If the master do not immediately adopt the new system in all the departments of his school, especially by teaching every letter, monosyllable, and the syllabic lessons of the spelling-book, by writing them on the slate, I shall entertain no good hope. Let him talk to me for ever of difficulties, want of room, etc., etc.,—he will talk in vain. . . . Difficulties in the instruction and discipline of a school are created by the master, or often handed down to him.

It leaves nothing more for me to do. All the world will in time learn every lesson by writing it. . . . It is completely done at the Barrington school; and all there think it all in all. I think it consummates my labours, and leaves nothing more for me to do.

(See D. Salmon ed., *Lancaster's Experiments and Bell's Improvements*, 1932.)

76

REPORT ON THE EDUCATION OF THE LOWER ORDERS, 1816–1818

Inspired by Lord Brougham, the radical Whig peer, this was the first attempt to investigate the general education field, and it painted a black picture of illiteracy and inadequate educational provision in London and elsewhere. The use of the Sunday school for teaching reading is apparent here, and the rector of St Clement Danes gives a clear view of the onerous problems involved with such low standards of living.

Evidence of the Rev. William Gurney, Rector of Saint Clement Danes.

Are you acquainted with the state of education among the lower orders in those parts of the town?

I know a great deal about it in Saint Giles's, because there I have the greatest establishment for children. . . . We found there were a great many who did not go to any school; the reason assigned in some measure for it was, their ragged condition, and their being unfit, from their great poverty, to appear decently at any school; and we found also, that a great many children went to Sunday schools belonging to Dissenters of various denominations, who had begun long before us to open schools; we found there was a very large Sunday school in Drury-lane, in which there were from 5 to 600 children; a very large number of our children I believe, went there. But there are a great many mendicants in our parish, owing to the extreme lowness of some parts of the neighbourhood, and the more children they have, the more success they meet with in begging, and they keep them in that way; so that in the weekday we could not get them to a day-school without some different measures were adopted; neither are they fit to appear in them as they are; and on a Sunday they get more by begging than they do on any other day in the week, because more people are out and about; we tried the experiment in several instances, by giving clothes to some of the most ragged, in order to bring them decent to school; they appeared for one Sunday or two, and then disappeared, and the clothes disappeared also. . . .

What is the annual expense of your Sunday school?

Very trifling; I have one collection a-year at the church, at which we generally get about £40; we do not go round to collect, it is a private thing done by the Teachers themselves; we have no master, or mistress, or any expense of that kind; the Teachers are all gratuitous and voluntary; the whole expense consists in the books and rent of the rooms; in fact now I have by great exertion got part of the vestry for a Sunday, which saves us the expense of paying rent.
Then the whole expense of this school does not exceed sixty or seventy pounds?
Seventy or eighty pounds; we give a good many rewards, according to our funds; and we have a writing school in the week, for the children who behave the best.
What hours do the children attend on a Sunday?
From about half-past eight or nine till twenty minutes before the church service commences in the morning, and again at two till five in the afternoon; we have not proper accommodation at the church for them, that is one great grievance to me; and if we had, we could have four times the number attend the school; we cannot accommodate them at the church, and I am forced to send a detachment of them to another chapel; I wanted to have a gallery erected; and I would have done it without any expense to the parish; two or three charity sermons would have done it.
How long does a child take, at the Sunday school, in learning to read, having no other instruction?
Several have learned to read in the course of about eighteen months; we would rather they would stay about two years, so as to be able to read a chapter in the testament; but others, of course, will take much longer, in consequence of the difference of abilities and attention. . . .
At what age do the children come to your school, generally?
We take them as soon as ever the boys have got breeches; we do not consult their age, but their size; we keep them till they are fit to go out; they generally leave us before they are twelve years of age; they are generally five years of age before we take them. I think altogether we have had four thousand children pass through the school during the last eight years; there are about three hundred out of the four hundred attend regularly; that is a very good proportion; and we are open to all parishes, without distinction.

REPORT ON THE STATE OF EDUCATION, 1834

By the eighteen-thirties, the first public grants for education had been paid to the National and British Societies. In 1834 another parliamentary inquiry showed that improvements had been made since the earlier years of the century, and that interest in education had quickened. This report is best known for its discussion of the various problems which were to prove irresolvable during the nineteenth century. The religious controversy, the training of teachers and methods of inspections were three such issues. Another was the position of the state. Lord Brougham, enthusiast for education though he was, still remained wary of central intervention.

Evidence of the Lord Chancellor, Lord Brougham and Vaux.

Do you consider that the aid or interference of the Legislature is required for promoting general education in this country?

I am of opinion that much may be done by judicious assistance; but legislative interference is in many respects to be either altogether avoided or very cautiously employed because it may produce mischievous effects.

Do you think that a system of primary education, established by law would be beneficial?

I think that it is wholly inapplicable to the present condition of the country, and the actual state of education. Those who recommend it on account of its successful adoption on the Continent, do not reflect upon the funds which it would require and upon the exertions already made in this country by individual beneficence. In 1818, there were half a million of children taught at day schools supported by voluntary contributions; and if I may trust the accuracy of returns which I received in 1828 from nearly 500 parishes taken at random all over the country, that number had more than doubled. It is probable that day schools for 1,200,000 at the least are now supported without endowment, and endowed schools are established for above 170,000, making, in all, schools capable of educating nearly 1,400,000, children. But if the state were to interfere, and obliged every parish to support a school or schools sufficient for educating all children, two consequences would inevitably follow; the greater part of the funds now raised voluntarily for this purpose

79

would be withdrawn and the State or the rate-payers in each parish would have to provide schools for 2,000,000 of children, because the interference would be quite useless, unless it supplied the whole defect, which is the difference between schools for one-tenth, the present amount, and schools for one-seventh, the amount required to educate the whole people. Now, to establish and maintain such a number of schools would be a most heavy expense. Suppose the average capacity of each to be 50 children, and the average number of those taught at the present unendowed day schools is under 35, there would be no less than 40,000 schools required, which, allowing only £50 a year for all expenses of salary and rent, would cost £2,000,000 a year. But supposing the expense were provided, I am clearly of opinion that one great means of promoting education would be lost, namely, the interest taken by the patrons of schools supported by voluntary contributions. . . . By degrees, as the parents themselves become better educated, the indifference to the advantage of schooling for their children will disappear. That the funds now raised by subscription, and which amount to near a million a year, will entirely fail, I take to be the inevitable consequence of establishing a school rate. All will think they do enough by paying that. . . . To which I must add, that my belief is, that a surer way to make education unpopular, and thus arrest its progress, could not be devised, than making it the cause either of a general tax, or of an increase in the parish rate.

JAMES KAY-SHUTTLEWORTH AND PUPIL TEACHERS, 1846

James Kay-Shuttleworth has a critical place in the story of Victorian social advancement. Perhaps his most enduring work was his scheme for pupil teaching, partly based on continental models he had observed. Its introduction really began the State's interest in teacher training and the pupil teacher was to remain throughout the century. The necessary qualifications illustrate the simple and mechanical nature of the schooling of the age, and they indicate the strong emphasis on moral and religious instruction. This excerpt is from the minutes of the committee of council on education established in 1839.

Pupil Teachers—Qualifications of Candidates. . . . They must be at least thirteen years of age, and must not be subject to any bodily infirmity likely to impair their usefulness. . . .

In schools connected with the Church of England, the clergyman and managers, and, in other schools, the managers must certify that the moral character of the candidates and of their families justify an expectation that the instruction and training of the school will be seconded by their own efforts and by the example of their parents. If this cannot be certified of the family the apprentice will be required to board in some approved household.

Candidates will also be required:

1. To read with fluency, ease and expression.
2. To write in a neat hand with correct spelling and punctuation, a simple prose narrative slowly read to them.
3. To write from dictation sums in the first four rules of arithmetic, simple and compound; to work them correctly, and know the table of weights and measures.
4. To point out the parts of speech in a simple sentence.
5. To have elementary knowledge of geography.
6. In schools connected with the Church of England they will be required to repeat the Catechism, and to show that they understand its meaning and are acquainted with the outline of Scripture history. The parochial clergyman will assist in this part of the examination.

In other schools the state of the religious knowledge will be certified by the managers.

7. To teach a junior class to the satisfaction of the Inspector.
8. Girls should also be able to sew neatly and to knit.

THE NEWCASTLE REPORT ON THE STATE OF POPULAR EDUCATION IN ENGLAND, 1861

This was the third famous report of the century on education, and it was by far the most richly documented and comprehensive. It offers a most full description of education in mid-century, and made several recommendations, few of which were adopted. Its chief consequence was Lowe's notorious revised code of the following year.

. . . The whole population of England and Wales, as estimated by the Registrar-General in the summer of 1858, amounted to 19,523,103. The number of children whose names ought, at the same date, to have been on the school books, in order that all might receive some education, was 2,655,767. The number we found to be actually on the books was 2,535,462, thus leaving 120,305 children without any school instruction whatever. The proportion, therefore, of scholars in week-day schools of all kinds to the entire population was 1 in 7·7 or 12·99 per cent. Of these 321,768 are estimated to have been above the condition of such as are commonly comprehended in the expression 'poorer classes', and hence are beyond the range of our present enquiry. Deducting these from the whole number of children on the books of some school, we find that 2,213,694 children belonging to the poorer classes were, when our statistics were collected and compiled, receiving elementary instruction in day schools. Looking, therefore, at mere numbers as indicating the state of popular education in England and Wales, the proportion of children receiving instruction to the whole population is, in our opinion, nearly as high as can be reasonably expected. The children do not, in fact, receive the kind of education they require. We have just noticed the extravagant disproportion between those who receive some education and those who receive a sufficient education. We know that the uninspected schools are in this respect far below the inspected; but even with regard to the inspected, we have seen overwhelming evidence from Her Majesty's Inspectors, to the effect that not more than one-fourth of the children receive a good education.

THE REVISED CODE, 1862

Robert Lowe's revised code introduced payment by results and, at one fell swoop, placed a tight screw on all levels of public educational expenditure. It was a most harsh scheme, but, while making for a somewhat soulless system, it attacked waste and extravagance directly. Scholars were examined by inspectors at various standards, and grants were graduated according to the level of their success coupled with attendance. Matthew Arnold was one H.M.I. who objected to 'the game of mechanical contrivances' and agitated for a more liberal approach to teaching, which, he felt, would be possible within a compulsory system. The 1882 standards were as follows.

	Standard I.	Standard II.	Standard III.
Reading.	Narrative in monosyllables.	One of the Narratives next in order after monosyllables in an elementary reading book used in the school.	A short paragraph from an elementary reading book used in the school.
Writing.	Form on blackboard or slate, from dictation, letters, capital and small manuscript.	Copy in manuscript character a line of print.	A sentence from the same paragraph, slowly read once, and then dictated in single words.
Arithmetic.	Form on blackboard or slate, from dictation, figures up to 20; name at sight figures up to 20; add and subtract figures up to 10, orally, from examples on blackboard.	A sum in simple addition or subtraction, and the multiplication table.	A sum in any simple rule as far as short division (inclusive).

	IV.	V.	VI.
Reading.	A short paragraph from a more advanced reading book used in the school.	A few lines of poetry from a reading book used in the first class of the school.	A short ordinary paragraph in a newspaper, or other modern narrative.
Writing.	A sentence slowly dictated once by a few words at a time, from the same book, but not from the paragraph read.	A sentence slowly dictated once, by a few words at a time, from a reading book used in the first class of the school.	Another short ordinary paragraph in a newspaper, or other modern narrative, slowly dictated once by a few words at a time.
Arithmetic.	A sum in compound rules (money).	A sum in compound rules (common weights and measures).	A sum in practice or bills of parcels.

THE CAMPAIGN FOR MUNICIPAL SCHOOLS, 1869

George Melly, a Northern M.P., in a speech to the House of Commons in 1869, typified the opinions of many at this stage. So inadequate were the facilities that the need for much more state or municipal interference was increasingly obvious, and Melly here argues the case for municipal schools. Like Arnold and other commentators, he was aware that lack of scholars not of schools was a major problem, which only compulsory attendance could correct.

In the first place I would build or buy free municipal schools, and plant them like Martello towers against the invading armies of pauperism and intemperance in the poorer districts of all our large towns. . . . I would give power to the schoolmaster of each school, (whom I would pay by numerical results,) by means of a school beadle, appointed by the master, or rather by the Municipal Council of Education, to summon and fine the parents of every child found, after fair notice, in the streets between the hours of 9 and 12 in the morning and 2 and 5 in the afternoon; and I would do nothing more, because nothing more would be required. Speaking on the authority of the Chief Constable of Liverpool, and of other men who have studied the subject, I believe that if you give such simple powers as these to the municipalities of our great cities, —if you begin, not with any Permissive Act, but by compelling Municipalities to rate themselves, and if you give the power of summoning the parent of any child not at school during school hours,—you will soon sweep the streets of the thousands of children now found in them. If you place that power in our hands we shall carry out it and thus fill the schools you have compelled us to erect.

With these three agencies, the certified industrial workhouse schools, the free schools, and the present denominational schools, we should approach to a solution of the problem. . . . We have a magnificent system of denominational schools, and by that system we are educating 1,500,000 of our children; and, as has been well said, there can be no doubt that the poorest class have a far better as well as a far cheaper education open to them than the poorer portion of the middle class. This is so; it is offered to them but they do not accept it; and the lower portion of the middle class and the upper section of the artisan class do accept it; and thus the existing schools are largely invaded by a class for whom neither the House of Commons nor private subscribers intended either grants or subscriptions. There is no question on which it would be more difficult to adduce statistics, still less to give names, but every one knows there are a large and increasing number of the well-to-do artisans and the smaller order of shopkeepers whose children attend these schools. As Eton, Harrow, and Rugby, built and endowed for the lower and middle classes, have been invaded by the rich, so the National primary schools have been invaded, and in some instances even monopolised, by classes for whom they were neither intended, nor are they now supported. And the Revised Code, to which I gave my hearty concurrence, has encouraged this state of things, and, by its inevitable working, has rather reduced the numbers of poor and neglected children who attend the National primary schools. The master, paid by results, prefers the well-dressed regularly attending children of a more respectable class, and the cold shoulder is not frequently given in the National Schools to the very children for whom they are endowed and maintained. On this very ground I am not afraid that these schools will not hold their ground.

In the next place the free municipal schools must necessarily be secular schools, because you cannot compel the ratepayers to subscribe for the teaching of a religious faith with which they do not agree. They must be secular, because you cannot compel the attendance of a child at a school where a creed is taught in which its parents do not believe. But this will be at once the very strength and safeguard of the present denominational schools. . . . I believe that a system of free secular municipal schools and compulsory attendance, far from doing any damage to, would give a great impetus in our large towns to the system of denominational schools; I believe that parents who now send their children to paying schools would not only continue to do so, but would send them in larger numbers, and pay higher fees; and thus, without injuring the existing schools, you would have solved the difficulty of ensuring the blessings of education to the whole population.

In conclusion, I have endeavoured to show the necessity for inquiry; to prove that the community desires, and that the Legislature has the right, the power, and the authority of precedent, to compel the education of the children for whose welfare it is responsible. . . . There is no cloud so dark and dangerous in our political horizon, no blot so foul upon our social system, no stain so deep upon the Christianity which we all profess, as the existence of . . . perhaps half a million children . . . who are growing to man's estate to be a curse instead of a blessing to the community in which they live—to be a cause of poverty, instead of a source of wealth, to the nation that has given them birth.

(G. Melly, *The Children of Liverpool and the Rural Schemes for National Education*, 1869.)

THE SCHOOL LOG-BOOK

The log book has long been a fixture in English schools. It records the life of the school, and it embraces the reports of visiting inspectors. There follows a set of short pieces from an old log-book, indicating how much a record illustrates curriculum, standards, methods and so on.

1862

Nov. 24th.   School inspected by the Revd. N. Gream. Half-holiday.

"   25th.   Usual progress. N.B. This kind of entry is specifically asked for in ' Instructions for Keeping the Log-book''.

"   27th.   Class examined by Revd. Mr Jones.

"   28th.   Ordinary progress.

1862. Copy of H. M. Inspector's (Rev. N. Gream) last Report, Received Dec. 19th.

'Boys'—   'This is a very efficient County School.'
'The attendance is necessarily irregular considering which attainments are very creditable.'

'Girls'—   'This school is conducted with much care by the Mistress, and the Needlework is particularly good, and of the most useful kind.'

1863

Feb. 23rd.   Usual Progress. Boy caned for refusing to take charge of a class, he is being unable to work in his own class lesson (Arithmetic); and again caned for shouting, as a threat, that he would 'go to Gateacre'.

1864

July 11th.   School opened with 31 in attendance.

Sept. 6th.   Very wet—Attendance only 21

1864. Copy of H.M.I.'s Report for 1864.

'Boys'—   'The instruction and order in this school are very fair for a Rural District where the boys are taken away for a great part of the year for agricultural purposes.'

'Girls & Infants'	'I am happy to be able to report well of this school. The order and attainments are very fair and much attention is paid to the sewing and cutting out.'

1864.
Feb. 22nd.   In consequence of the Home Lessons taking up so much time in hearing and examining I do not commence the time-table routine till from 9.30 to 9.40 each morning. I consider the home lessons more than a recompense for the irregularity they cause.

Oct. 25th.   Drill in silence.

1866.
March 19th.   1st and 2nd class examined and passed well in Catechism.

"   20th.   3rd class examined in Catechism—answered very poorly, the monitor admonished.

"   21st.   4th class heard in Reading.

"   22nd.   4th class heard in Arithmetic—still backward.

"   26th.   1st class examined in Rdg. Jas. Lawrenson manages the subject but poorly.

July 24th.   In consequence of information received for Revd. J. Chambers that the Fourth Standard will have their sums set in words, not in figures by the Inspector, I have today examined and found that the Fourth standard boys are behind in numeration.

1870.
Oct. 5th   Usual progress. Took particular pains to teach the first class parsing.

"   11th.   Grammar and Geography to first class.

"   19th.   Gave lesson on numeration and one on Geography, Mathematical, Physical Political.

"   21st.   Requested the attendance of all on Monday week, the day of the inspection. Went through the Old Testament History.

"   Examination—Present 65. Number presented for examination 57 and 3 Standard VII. Four absent.

Number attended above 200 times 65. Presented 16 in Grammar and Geography. The Rector examined the first class in the Acts of the Apostles, the reigns of Saul, David and Solomon. After the examination the band played several times for the Inspector. He also heard the boys sing.

Nov. 4th — Lesson on Gunpowder plot in the afternoon. Began reading English history with the first division of the first class.

1870. — Copy of Her Majesty's Inspectors' Report for 1870.

'Boys' — 'The boys are well taught and in good order.'
'The School Band performed admirably.'

'Girls' — 'The school is orderly and the results of the examination are satisfactory.'

1871.
Dec. 7th. — Received from the Inspector by the Rector the following.

Syllabus of Examination in English History for 1872.

Standard IV. In outline, the early History of England the Saxons and Normans.

Standard V. As in Standard IV with the reign of Alfred, pretty well—outlines of Norman Conquest particularly.

Standard VI. All in Standards IV and V. Magna Charta particularly.

1872.
Jan. 23rd. — Admitted Joseph Radley—Wrote out the Roman Period in English History on the blackboard.

Feb. 2nd. — School visited by the Rector who brought the following passage for Dictation:—

'It is agreeable to perceive the unparalleled embarrassment of a harassed pedlar gauging the symmertry (sic) of a peeled pear.'

The least number of mistakes were four obtained by Christopher Horton in Standard V.

Feb. 19th. — Ordinary progress. Standards V and VI Dictations and Reading from newspaper.

1885.
Dec. 15th.   Average attendance 76.
1886.
Feb. 8th.   Francis Lawrenson in Standard VII commenced
                     as a paid monitor.
April 12th.   The monitor Francis Lawrenson was absent all
                     week from illness.
   "   19th.   Monitor Francis Lawrenson still absent from
                     illness.

REPORT FOR 1886

The master has since January been working single handed. His
assistant became a student in a Training College and the candidate
who was to have taken his place has been withdrawn owing to bad
health. It is not surprising therefore to find some falling off both in
the quality of the work and the number of passes.

The master cannot fairly be blamed and indeed deserves credit
for the results he has obtained in spite of his difficulties. The reading
is too monotonous and unintelligent to be considered satisfactory.
Spelling in fourth standard is weak and composition is of unequal
quality. Arithmetic is, except in the fourth standard where weights
and measures are not well known, and in the sixth standard in which
fractions are not well mastered, accurate and intelligent.

The higher rate of payment is recommended for English, but only
the lower for Geography, the third, fifth (this class in map drawing)
and sixth standards doing badly.

                                   Thos. Chambers M.A.
                                   Corresponding Man.

(Taken from the log-book of a Lancashire rural church school).

W. E. FORSTER AND THE 1870 ACT

Parts of the speech by W. E. Forster in the House of Commons introducing his great education bill is a fitting illustration of the initiation of a full-scale public system of education. It is an extract which speaks for itself, but it also recalls the value of Hansard to the researcher. Educational debates are often full both of rich polemical material and thoughtful, philosophic ideas.

More or less imperfectly about 1,500,000 children are educated in the schools that we help—that is, they are simply on the registers. But, as I had the honour of stating last year, only two-fifths of the children of the working classes between the ages of six and ten years are on the registers of the Government schools, and only one-third of those between the ages of ten and twelve. Consequently, of those between six and ten, we have helped about 700,000 more or less, but we have left unhelped 1,000,000; while of those between ten and twelve, we have helped 250,000, and left unhelped at least 500,000. . . . Our object is to complete the present voluntary system, to fill up gaps, sparing the public money where it can be done without, procuring as much as we can the assistance of the parents, and welcoming as much as we rightly can the co-operation and aid of those benevolent men who desire to assist their neighbours.

Now I will at once proceed to the main principles that run through all our clauses for securing efficient school provision. They are two in number. Legal enactment, that there shall be efficient schools everywhere throughout the kingdom. Compulsory provision of such schools if and where needed, but not unless proved to be needed. These being the principles, I now come to the actual provisions.

The first provision that would probably suggest itself to the minds of all hon. members would be a system of organisation throughout the country. We take care that the country shall be properly mapped and divided, so that its wants may be duly ascertained. For this, we take present known division, and declare them to be school districts, so that upon the passing of this Bill there will be no portion of England or Wales not included in one school district or another. . . .

The school boards are to provide the education. Who are to pay for it? In the first place, shall we give up the school fees? I know that some earnest friends of education would do that. I at once say that the Government are not prepared to do it. If we did so the sacrifice would be enormous. The parents paid in school fees last year about £420,000. If this scheme works, as I have said we hope it will work, it will very soon cover the country, and that £420,000 per annum would have to be doubled, or even trebled. Nor would it stop there. This would apply to the elementary education chiefly of the working classes. The middle classes would step in—the best portion of the working classes would step in—and say, 'There must be free education also for us, and that free education must not be confined to elementary schools'. The illustration and example, so often quoted, of America would be quoted again, and we should be told that in the New England States education is free not only in the elementary schools, but free also up to the very highest education of the State. The cost would be such as really might well alarm my right hon. friend the Chancellor of the Exchequer. I hope the country would be ready to incur that cost if necessary; but I think it would be not only unnecessary, but mischievous. Why should we relieve the parent from all payments for the education of his child? We come in and help the parents in all possible ways; but, generally speaking, the enormous majority of them are able, and will continue to be able, to pay these fees. Nevertheless, we do take two powers. We give the school board power to establish special free schools under special circumstances which chiefly apply to large towns, where, from the exceeding poverty of the district, or for other very special reasons, they prove to the satisfaction of the Government that such a school is needed, and ought to be established. . . .

We also empower the school board to give free tickets to parents who they think really cannot afford to pay for the education of their children; and we take care that those free tickets shall have no stigma of pauperism attached to them. We do not give up the school fees, and indeed we keep to the present proportions—namely, of about one-third raised from the parents, one-third out of the public taxes, and one-third out of local funds. Where the local funds are not raised by voluntary subscription the rates will come into action. . . .

I have said that this is a very serious question; I would further say that whatever we do in the matter should be done quickly. We must not delay. Upon the speedy provision of elementary education depends our industrial prosperity. It is of no use trying to give technical teaching to our artisans without elementary education; uneducated labourers—and many of our labourers are utterly uneducated—are, for the most part, unskilled labourers, and if we leave our work-folk any longer unskilled, notwithstanding their strong sinews and determined energy, they will become over-matched in the competition of the world. . . . Upon this speedy provision of education depends also our national power. Civilized communities throughout the world are massing themselves together, each mass being measured by its force; and if we are to hold our position among men of our own race or among the nations of the world we must make up the smallness of our numbers by increasing the intellectual force of the individual.

(Hansard, 17th February, 1870.)

THE LIVERPOOL SCHOOL BOARD

The Liverpool School Board was one of the earliest and one of the largest to be formed. The first part of this extract is the complete return to the state authority of educational provision in Liverpool. Every area had to make this return in order for the 'gaps' to be diagnosed. The second section outlines some of the local bye-laws, by which it was possible, for instance, to establish compulsory education and assist with fees. The third piece defines the curriculum with its 'essential' and 'discretionary' subjects. Give or take one or two subjects and an odd change of name, and the timetable was not too unlike that of today.

ELEMENTARY EDUCATION ACT, 1870.

MUNICIPAL BOROUGH OF LIVERPOOL

General Return with respect to the population, rating, and school provision within the municipal limits of the borough, comprising the parish of Liverpool, the townships of Everton and Kirkdale, and parts of the townships of West Derby and Toxteth Park.

N.B. This return is to be strictly confined to the area within the municipal limits of the borough. If any parish is divided by these limits, the part without the municipal area will be dealt with separately. This return is to include only the parts of such parishes within that area.

I. This borough by the census of 1861 contained 443,938 inhabitants.

II. It is estimated that the population now amounts to 517,567.

III. The rateable value of the borough is by the rate books now in force (dated 1870) £2,677,559.

IV. The number of ratepayers, duly rated under the provisions of the Poor Rate Assessment and Collection Act, 1869, is 94,266.

V. The number of elementary schools, for which returns are herewith made to the Education Department is:—

    (a) In operation....................223
    (b) In course of being supplied 14
           Total 237

N.B. It will be very convenient if you can forward with the return a map of the borough, with the position of these schools marked upon it.

VI. The number of the schools to which forms of return were delivered, but which have omitted or refused to fill them up, is 45. A list of these schools is filed herewith.

I, the undersigned, Town Clerk and Clerk to the School Board of the Borough of Liverpool, by the authority and with the approval of the Town Council of the said Borough, hereby certify to the completeness and accuracy of this general return.

Signed, this 31st day of December, 1870.

Joseph Rayner, Town Clerk, and
Clerk to the School Board, Liverpool.

BYE-LAWS REFERRED TO IN THE FOREGOING ORDER

Recital of 74th section of Education Act, authorising School Boards to make Bye-Laws as to attendance at school.

Whereas, by the 74th section of the Elementary Education Act, 1870, it is enacted that every School Board may, from time to time, with the approval of the Education Department, make Bye-Laws for all or any of the following purposes:

1. Requiring the parents of children of such age, not less than five years nor more than thirteen years, as may fixed by the Bye-Laws, to cause such children (unless there is some reasonable excuse) to attend school.

2. Determining the time during which children are so to attend school, provided that no such Bye-Laws shall prevent the withdrawal of any child from any religious observance or instruction in religious subjects, or shall require any child to attend school on any day exclusively set apart for religious observance by the religious body to which his parent belongs, or shall be contrary to anything contained in any Act for regulating the education of children employed in labour.

3. Providing for the remission or payment of the whole or any part of the fees of any child, where the parent satisfies the School Board that he is unable from poverty to pay the same.

4. Imposing penalties for the breach of any Bye-Laws.

5. Revoking or altering any Bye-Laws previously made.

Provided that any Bye-Law under this section requiring a child between ten and thirteen years of age to attend school shall provide for the total or partial exemption of such child from the obligation to attend school, if one of Her Majesty's Inspectors certifies that such child has reached a standard of education specified in such Bye-Law.

General Purposes Committee of the Liverpool School Board, 1871

III. REGULATIONS FOR JUNIOR AND SENIOR SCHOOLS

9. Senior schools shall be separate.

10. Junior schools, pending the final decision of the Board, may be experimentally either mixed or separate.

11. In junior schools, whether mixed or separate, female teachers may be advantageously employed.

12. In senior boys' schools the teachers shall be males.

13. In senior girls' schools the teachers shall be female.

14. In junior and senior schools certain kinds of instruction shall form an essential part of the teaching of every school but others may be added to them by special direction of the Board. The instruction in discretionary subjects shall not interfere with the efficiency of the teaching of the essential subjects.

15. The following subjects shall be ESSENTIAL:

   (a) Religious teaching, in accordance with the terms of the resolution of the Board passed on the 17th July, 1871.

   (b) Reading, writing and arithmetic.

   (c) English grammar and composition.

   (d) History.

   (e) Geography.

   (f) Vocal music and drill.

   (g) In girls' schools plain needlework and cutting out.

16. The following subjects shall be DISCRETIONARY:

   (a) The principles of book-keeping.

   (b) Elementary drawing.

   (c) Systematised object-lessons, serving as an introduction to

   (d) Elementary instruction in physical science, together with such other branches of education as the Board may from time to time find it desirable to introduce.

H.M.I.—AN INSPECTOR'S MEMOIRS

H.M.I. is the name of the memoirs of E. M. Sneyd-Kynnersley, who was an inspector for many years during the later decades of the nineteenth century. It was published in 1913. *His experience covered both urban and rural areas, and the book is an amusing and shrewd example of how valuable such memoirs can be.*

The advantage of the School Board system was that it provided a body of men who had an opportunity of being acquainted with the wants of the place; usually qualified by residence to attend meetings; and with large powers of raising money to carry on the work.

The disadvantage was that it put technical, skilled labour into the hands of men from whom no proof of skill was required; and in very many places into the hands of men who were manifestly skill-less. In the large towns the Board might become a Debating Society, but if it escaped this snare, it often did well. In small villages sometimes it was a farce, sometimes a tragedy. In most places, whether large or small, the real power fell into the hands of one man, either the clerk or the chairman, who managed both School Board and Board School.

Do you ask for an instance? At a Board School inspection, noticing that there were not enough desks for the children, I asked the chairman, who was present, to see that the deficiency was made good at once. He assured me that it would be done without delay.

'When does the Board meet?' I asked.

'Oh, we don't meet: I get what is wanted and then on market-day I go down to the town, where I am sure to find the members; they are all farmers. I say to Brown, 'The Inspector was here last week; wants some more desks; always asking for something; suppose you agree?' And he says, 'Whatever you think is right, Mr Chairman'. Then I go on to Jones, and Robinson, and Snooks, and they all agree. We don't bother about a meeting, except once a year to make Form IX for your inspection.'

What admirable discipline!

The absolute unfitness for any educational work of some Boards led to strange results. Somewhere in Wales I had sent notice to a Board that I proposed to meet them at a certain place on a certain day. They sent no answer, but I kept my own appointment, and found the Board duly assembled. I began by suggesting that it was usual to answer official letters. They declared they did not know where I lived, and how could they send a letter? I pointed out that the official notepaper, upon which I wrote, had the address printed at the top. This embarrassed them: but the true explanation was given to me afterwards. There was not a man on the Board who could read and write, and they had to take all their correspondence to the market-town to get the advice of the Clerk to the Guardians before they could reply. They were in too small a way of educational business to have a clerk of their own. . . .

Another Board annually stirred me to mirthful compassion, because I knew, and none other knew, that it owed its birth to defective arithmetic. The parish had a population of several thousands; when the school accommodation and requirements were compared in the early 'seventies, a nought got wrong, as noughts will do at times, and a deficit of 130 places was announced. The real deficit was 13, but it was no one's business to check the figures, and 130 prevailed. The parish declined to build, and a School Board was duly elected. It spent the next ten years in pointing out to the Department in London that no new school was wanted; and My Lords unwillingly agreed: but no one found out about the nought. And it was a very useful Board, and, like the young man, Godfrey Bertram Hewitt, in *Guy Mannering*, was 'in a fair way of doing well in the world, although he came somewhat irregularly into it'.

THE BRYCE REPORT ON SECONDARY EDUCATION, 1895

The Bryce report foreshadowed the 1902 Act, for it recommended a coherent and uniform organisation and implied the need for a humane approach to secondary education. The Cockerton judgment and Balfour's Act, with Morant fencing skilfully in the background, followed hard on its heels.

In dwelling on the need for a systematic organisation of Secondary Education we have more than once had occasion to explain that we mean by 'system' neither uniformity nor the control of a Central Department of government. Freedom, variety, elasticity are, and have been, the merits which go far to redeem the defects in English education, and they must at all hazards be preserved. The 'system' which we desire to see introduced may rather be described as coherence, an organic relation between different authorities and different kinds of schools which will enable each to work with due regard to the work to be done by the others, and will therewith avoid waste both of effort and of money. Of the loss now incurred through the want of such coherence and correlation, it is impossible to speak too strongly. It is the fault on which all our witnesses and all our Assistant Commissioners unite in dwelling. Unfortunately, so far from tending to cure itself, it is an evil which every day strikes its roots deeper. The existing authorities and agencies whose want of cooperation we lament are each of them getting more accustomed to the exercise of their present powers, and less disposed to surrender them. Vested interests are being created which will stand in the way of the needed reforms. Instances occur in which large sums of money are being expended in buildings, or otherwise upon institutions, which, if not superfluous, are planned upon imperfect lines, and with reference to one area or one purpose only where others should have been equally regarded. . . . Thus the difficulty of introducing the needful coherence and correlation becomes constantly greater, and will be more serious a year or two hence than it is at this moment.

Elementary education is among the first needs of a people, and especially of a free people, as appears by the fact that all, or nearly all, modern constitutional States have undertaken to provide it. But it is by those who have received a further and superior kind of instruction that the intellectual progress of a nation is maintained. It is they who provide its literature, who advance its science, who direct its government. In England, those classes which have been wont to resort to the universities have, during the last sixty or seventy years, fared well. Those who could afford to pay the very high charges made at some of the great endowed schools have had an education which, if somewhat one-sided, has been highly stimulative to certain types of mind. But the great body of the commercial and professional classes were long forced to content themselves with a teaching which was usually limited in range and often poor in quality, and whose defects had become so familiar that they had ceased to be felt as defects.

Things have improved within the last thirty years, as may be seen by whoever compares the picture drawn by our Assistant Commissioners with that contained in the reports of the Assistant Commissioners of 1865. But the educational opportunities offered in most of our towns, and in nearly all our country districts, to boys or girls who do not proceed to the universities, but leave school at sixteen, are still far behind the requirements of our time, and far less ample than the incomes of the parents and the public funds available might well provide.

Not a few censors have dilated upon the disadvantages from which young Englishmen suffer in industry and commerce owing to the superior preparation of their competitors in several countries of continental Europe. These disadvantages are real. But we attach importance to the faults of dullness and barrenness to which so many lives are condemned by the absence of those capacities for intellectual enjoyment which ought to be awakened in youth. In an age of increasing leisure and luxury, when men have more time and opportunity for pleasure, and pursue it more eagerly, it becomes all the more desirable that they should be induced to draw it from the best sources. Thus, it is not merely in the interest of the material prosperity and intellectual activity of the nation, but no less in that of its happiness and its moral strength, that the extension and reorganisation of Secondary Education seem entitled to a place among the first subjects with which social legislation ought to deal.

THE LIVERPOOL EDUCATION COMMITTEE, 1902

The Liverpool school board was used as an instance of the workings of the 1870 Act, and here is the constitution of its successor established under the 1902 Act. It should be noted that the area of jurisdiction was exactly the same. Another point of interest is that both school boards and education committees were obliged to have women members—some years before female suffrage had been accepted.

CITY OF LIVERPOOL

EDUCATION ACT, 1902

Scheme of the Council of the City of Liverpool for the constitution of an Education Committee under the provisions of the Education Act, 1902.

1. The Committee shall be a Committee of the City Council of Liverpool, and shall be called 'The Education Committee'.
2. The Education Committee (hereinafter called 'The Committee') shall consist of 52 members, and shall be constituted as follows:

18 members shall be appointed by the City Council from amongst the Members of that body, and

18 members, at least three of whom shall be women, shall be appointed by the City Council as hereinafter provided.

The Committee shall include, in addition to persons experienced in Technical and Elementary Education and persons acquainted with the needs of the various kinds of Schools in the City, persons directly engaged in and representative of the commerce, trade, industries and professions of the City.

3. The following bodies shall have the right to recommend persons as Members of the Committee, viz.:

	Number to be Recommended
The Council of University College, Liverpool, or of the University of Liverpool	2
The Liverpool United Trades and Labour Council	1

Associations representing the different kinds of Voluntary Schools, that is to say:

(a) An Association recognised by the Council for the purpose comprising the Church of England Elementary Schools within the City of Liverpool — 2

(b) An Association recognised by the Council for the purpose comprising the Roman Catholic Schools within the City of Liverpool — 1

(c) Associations recognised by the Council for the purpose representing Wesleyan and other Voluntary Schools within the City of Liverpool not hereinbefore provided for — 1

The Governing Bodies of the different kinds of Public Secondary Schools — 3 one of whom shall be a woman

Liverpool and Districts Teachers' Association of the National Union of Teachers — 1

The Liverpool School Board in the case of the first Committee. For subsequent committees such members shall be appointed by the City Council — 4 one of whom shall be a woman

The City Council shall also appoint from amongst persons experienced in Technical and Elementary Education and persons acquainted with the needs of the various kinds of Schools in the City — 3 at least one of whom shall be a woman

—

18

EDUCATION IN THE NINETEEN-HUNDREDS

As a final extract, it would seem proper to quote from the H.M.S.O. booklet
Education 1900–1950, *which begins with a resume of the origins and
early workings of the 1902 Act. The booklet then goes on to survey education
in the first half of the twentieth century, and is a useful guide to readers
wishing to see how this century's educational administrators built on the work
of their predecessors. It also exemplifies the value of H.M.S.O. publications
for the student of education.*

THE NEED FOR LEGISLATION

6. There were thus three separate strands of secondary education
(though the phrase was as yet rarely used) in 1900: the endowed
schools under the care of the Charity Commissioners, the higher
grade or higher top elementary schools, whether voluntary or
Board, drawing grant from the Education Department in Whitehall,
and science 'schools' or classes drawing grant from the Science and
Art Department and located indiscriminately in grammar schools,
higher grade schools and evening continuation schools. There was
much confusion and overlapping between the central departments
and no co-ordination in the field itself. The problem was how to
weave these three strands into a single system—a problem, in-
cidentally, that was not to be solved until 1944.

7. Matthew Arnold had long urged the necessity for such a system.
Appalled by the unfavourable comparison between secondary
education in England and in most continental countries, he had
been the moving spirit behind not only the Schools Inquiry Commission but also the Bryce Commission on Secondary Education,
although he died before the latter's report was published in 1895.
That report recommended the establishment of a single central
authority 'not in order to control but rather to supervise education
in this country'. Hence the establishment of the Board of Education
in 1900. The Bryce Report also advocated the creation of new local
authorities in every county and every county borough for providing
secondary education. The latter recommendation, which was not,
of course, adopted, side-stepped one of the burning questions of
the day—should secondary education be entrusted to the School

Boards or to the county councils, county boroughs and lesser local authorities?

8. The Education Act of 1902 came down on the side of local authorities. It charged the county councils and county borough councils (but not the borough and urban district councils, the authorities for Part III of the Act) to 'consider the educational needs of their areas and to take such steps as seemed to them desirable, after consultation with the Board of Education, to supply or aid the supply of education other than elementary'. In other words the Act encouraged, but did not compel, local authorities to provide higher, or secondary, education out of the rates.

9. Although the demand for educational reform was fairly general by the end of the century, there were serious difficulties in the way of introducing the necessary legislation. Any system of secondary education, to be successful, must be based on a sound elementary system. The existing one was badly in need of overhaul, and to Sir Robert Morant, the architect of the 1902 Act, it was clear that this involved two things: first, the abolition of the School Boards, and, secondly, the aiding of the voluntary schools out of the rates; for voluntary schools, which were nearly three times as numerous as the Board schools, were in urgent need of financial support. Both these proposals aroused fierce opposition—the former from the Boards themselves and their supporters, of whom Joseph Chamberlain was one, the latter from the powerful Nonconformist interests.

ADMINISTERING THE NEW SYSTEM

12. Morant also left his mark on the elementary schools. The Elementary School Code of 1904, which was largely his work, founded a policy in marked contrast to the old system of 'payment by results'. The prefatory note in particular, though it necessarily reflected the current conception of elementary education as being for the masses and secondary education only for the gifted few, broke new ground, and in a sense may be said to have anticipated the 1944 Act, by the emphasis it placed on the potentialities of the individual child. As a statement of aims it is still largely valid, and it was repeated in every edition of the Code until 1926, and thereafter in the Board's *Handbook of Suggestions for Teachers*. The opening sentence well conveys the spirit of the whole:

'The purpose of the Public Elementary School is to form and strengthen the character and to develop the intelligence of the children entrusted to it, and to make the best use of the school years available, in assisting both girls and boys, according to their different needs, to fit themselves, practically as well as intellectually, for the work of life.'

13. During the years of energetic and fruitful administration that continued until the first world war the new organisation became consolidated. 'All the partners in the work of education', it has been written, 'were new and had to learn their job and get to know each other. The Board of Education soon realised the limitations of its powers and chose the path of leading rather than dictating. The new local education authorities got down to the business of surveying their areas and preparing schemes to remedy deficiencies, and the managers of the non-provided and endowed schools took their responsibilities seriously and did much to improve the schools under their charge.'

Bibliography

GENERAL

Some readers may wish to study English education as a segment of the whole history of education. (**1**) E. D. Myers, *Education in the Perspective of History*, Harper, 1960 offers such a survey on a grand scale, while, for a slightly less wide-ranging canvas, (**2**) W. Boyd, *The History of Western Education*, Black, 1921 (7th ed., 1964) has become the classic exposition of education in Western society from the Greeks onwards. (**3**) T. L. Jarman, *Landmarks in the History of Education*, Cresset Press, 1951, selects the major steps in educational development and treats them shrewdly and (**4**) R. H. Beck, *A Social History of Education*, Prentice-Hall, 1965, sees education as a manifestation of social history, albeit with a strong American bias in the later sections. (**5**) E. B. Castle, *Ancient Education and Today*, Penguin, 1961 is an eminent account of the relevance of the educational problems of antiquity to our own. (**6**) N. Hans, *Comparative Education*, Routledge and Kegan Paul, 1950 and (**7**) E. J. King, *World Perspectives in Education*, Rinehart, 1962, and (**8**) *Other Schools and Ours*, Rinehart, 1958 (2nd edition, 1963) are perhaps the soundest and most helpful investigations of comparative education. (**9**) J. S. Brubacher, *History of the Problems of Education*, McGraw-Hill, 1947. (**10**) H. G. Good, *A History of Western Education*, Collier-MacMillan, 1947 and (**11**) R. F. Butts, *A Cultural History of Education*, McGraw-Hill, 1947, are three further valuable general studies.

Education has always attracted the philosopher and the writer, and the number of educational tracts from Plato to the present are legion. Boyd (**2**) has a helpful bibliography, and (**12**) S. J. Curtis and M. E. A. Boultwood, *A Short History of Educational Ideas*, University Tutorial Press, 1953 or (**13**) J. Adams, *The Evolution of Educational Theory*, Macmillan, 1912, trace the philosophic development of education admirably. (**14**) R. R. Rusk, *The Doctrines of the Great Educators*, Macmillan, 1954, adopts a readable biographical slant, while a useful compendium of extracts, neatly arranged under topics, is provided by (**15**) A. Cohen and N. Garner, *Readings in Educational Thought*, London University Press, 1967.

Turning to the general background of English education, (**16**) G. O. Trevelyan, *Illustrated English Social History*, Longmans, 1942 (illustrated edition, 1949, 3rd ed. 1960; also Penguin 1964) is still probably the most pleasing introduction. For a more specifically nineteenth-century picture, (**17**) L. Woodward, *The Age of Reform 1815–1870*, 1938 Oxford University Press and (**18**) R. Ensor, *England, 1870–1914*, Oxford University Press, 1936, are comprehensive and rewarding. Both have good bibliographies.

Works dealing with the era prior to the nineteenth century include, of course, sections of those already mentioned. Readers needing a succinct outline of the origins of industrialism might turn to (**19**) T. S. Ashton, *The Industrial Revolution*, Oxford University Press, 1948, (9th edition, 1960). (**20**) M. G. Jones, *The Charity School Movement*, Cass, 1938, is accepted as the premier work in that important field, while (**21**) W. K. Jordan, *The Charities of London, 1480–1660*, Allen & Unwin, 1960 and (**22**) *The Charities of Rural England*, Allen & Unwin, 1961, are the most up-to-date examinations of the general basis of charitable education provision in Tudor and Stuart times. As Tudor education was particularly mentioned in this monograph, (**23**) G. Davies, *The Enforcement of English Apprenticeships*, Harvard, 1956, might be recommended. In that educational and social reform are closely linked, some readers may like to regard (**24**) E. C. Midwinter, *Victorian Social Reform*, Longmans, 1968, as a companion volume to this.

Probably the finest work to turn to on this subject, however, is (**25**) W. A. G. Armytage, *Four Hundred Years of English Education*, Cambridge University Press, 1965. This supplies a general context before, during and after the nineteenth century, and its specialist touch is always skilled and entertaining. The book concludes with a set of lively notes from which a most exhilarating bibliography may be devised.

THE NINETEENTH CENTURY

A number of histories of English public education are available. Among the best known are (**26**) H. C. Barnard, *A Short History of*

English Education, 1760–1944, London University Press, 1947, (**27**) F. Smith, *A History of English Elementary Education 1760–1902*, University of London, 1931; (**28**) S. J. Curtis, *History of Education in Great Britain*, University Tutorial Press, 1953, and (**29**) A. D. C. Peterson, *A Hundred Years of Education*, Duckworth, 1952.

Sometimes these, however, tend to emphasise the legal, theoretical and constitutional aspects of education, although they are all, in their fashion, admirable. For a more richly social view (**30**) B. Simon, *Studies in the History of Education, 1780–1870*, Lawrence & Wishart, 1960 and (**31**) *Education and the Labour Movement*, Lawrence & Wishart, 1965, are highly recommended. Simon's books stress the working-class position with sympathy and meaning. If antidote be needed, a brief but significant one is provided by (**32**) H. J. Perkin, 'Middle-class education and employment in the nineteenth century: a critical note', *Economic History Review*, xiv (1961).

Apart from these, any number of special studies exist. (**33**) D. Salmon ed., *Lancaster's Improvements and Bell's Experiments*, Cambridge University Press, 1932, is probably the most simple and invigorating account of monitorialism, which has been rather neglected in recent years. The promotion of private secondary schools is dealt with by (**34**) H. J. Burgess, *Enterprise in Education*, National Society and S.P.C.K., 1958, and (**35**) G. Ward, 'Education of factory child workers 1833-1850', *Economic Journal Supplement* (1935) handles that aspect of early Victorian schooling. Thomas Arnold has attracted a host of biographers of whom one of the latest (**36**) T. W. Bamford, *Thomas Arnold*, Cresset Press, 1960 is perhaps the most objective. His son, Matthew, of course, is famous for his own writings, such as (**37**) *Culture and Anarchy*, (1861), Murray, 1962, but a notable assessment of his work may be found in (**38**) W. F. Connell, *The Educational Thought and Influence of Matthew Arnold*, Routledge & Kegan Paul, 1950. (**39**) F. Smith, *Life of Sir James Kay Shuttleworth*, Murray, 1923, and (**40**) B. M. Allen *Sir Robert Morant*, Macmillan, 1934, are biographies of two other celebrated Victorian educational administrators.

The church problem is covered by (**41**) M. Cruickshank, *Church and State in English Education: 1870 to the present day*, Macmillan, 1963. Of great value is (**42**) J. Murphy, *The Religious Problem in English Education. The crucial experiment*, Liverpool University Press, 1959, which deals with Liverpool's early attempt at municipal schooling and the religious issues raised by it. (**43**) N. Ball, *Her Majesty's*

Inspectorate, 1839–1849, Oliver & Boyd, 1963; (**44**) H. M. Pollard, *Pioneers in Popular Education*, Murray, 1956; (**45**) A. Tropp, *The School Teachers*, Heinemann, 1957, and (**46**) T. Kelly, *A History of Adult Education in Great Britain*, Liverpool University Press, 1962 are other stimulating specialist works.

The era of governmental activity in education after 1870 has given rise to a series of closely analysed and well-detailed studies. (**47**) E. J. R. Eaglesham, *From School Board to Local Authority*, Routledge & Kegan Paul, 1956, surveys with exceptional insight the character of school boards and their transition to L.E.As. (**48**) G. A. N. Lowndes, *The Silent Social Revolution*, Oxford University Press, 1937, (**49**) R. Williams, *The Long Revolution*, Chatto & Windus, 1961, and (**50**) A. V. Judges, ed., *Pioneers of English Education*, Faber, 1952 are other most vitally interesting and critical works.

EDUCATION TODAY

Some students may wish to follow up their Victorian studies with contemporary reading. The following short list suggests several of the more important and valuable books. (**51**) M. L. Jacks, *Modern Trends in Education*, Melrose, 1952, (**52**) F. Clarke, *Education and Social Change*, Sheldon Press, 1943; (**53**) K. Mannheim, *Diagnosis of Our Time*, Routledge & Kegan Paul, 1940, (**54**) A. K. C. Ottoway, *Education and Society: an introduction to the sociology of education*, Routledge & Kegan Paul, 1953; (**55**) S. J. Curtis, *Education in Britain since 1900*, Dakers, 1952; (**56**) H. C. Dent, *The Education Act 1944*, London University Press, 1947; (**57**) W. O. Lester Smith, *Education*, Penguin, 1957 and (**58**) *Government of Education*, Penguin, 1965; (**59**) T. Burgess, *A Guide to English Schools*, Penguin, 1964 and (**60**) J. Vaizey, *Education for Tomorrow*, Penguin, 1962. As for comprehensive schooling, (**61**) R. Pedley, *The Comprehensive School*, Penguin, 1959, states the issues clearly, whereas (**62**) M. Young, *The Rise of the Meritocracy*, Thomas and Hudson, 1958 (also Penguin 1961) and (**63**) E. James, *Education and Democratic Leadership*, Harrap, 1951, argue the case against and for an elite chosen by education.

Her Majesty's Stationery Office publish numerous papers and reports on education, among which (**64**) *Education 1900–1950*, H.M.S.O., 1951, is particularly informative. But of immense value for ease of reference and substantial content is (**65**) J. S. Maclure, *Educational Documents, England and Wales, 1816–1963*, Chapman & Hall, 1965. This fine anthology of extracts could well serve as a fitting introduction to and commentary on the foregoing section of documents.

Index

DATE DUE

FE 12'82			
FE 26'82			
MR 17'82			
FEB 23'87			
MAR 17'87			
GAYLORD			PRINTED IN U.S.A.